The Gentle Barbarian

Also by BOHUMIL HRABAL

FROM NEW DIRECTIONS

All My Cats

I Served the King of England

*Mr. Kafka and Other Tales
from the Time of the Cult*

THE GENTLE
BARBARIAN

Bohumil Hrabal

*Translated from the Czech
by Paul Wilson*

A NEW DIRECTIONS
PAPERBOOK ORIGINAL

Originally published in Czech as *Něžný barbar* in 1974

First published by New Directions in 2021
Manufactured in the United States of America
Design by Erik Rieselbach

Library of Congress Cataloging-in-Publication Data
Names: Hrabal, Bohumil, 1914–1997, author. | Wilson, Paul, translator.
Title: The gentle barbarian : a pedagogical text / Bohumil Hrabal ;
translated from the Czech by Paul Wilson.
Other titles: Něžný barbar. English
Description: First edition. | New York : New Directions Publishing, 2021.
Identifiers: LCCN 2020043603 | ISBN 9780811228589 (paperback) |
ISBN 9780811228596 (ebook)
Subjects: LCSH: Boudník, Vladimír, 1924–1968. |
Czechoslovakia – Social life and customs.
Classification: LCC NX571.C94 B683413 2021 | DDC 700.9 – dc23
LC record available at https://lccn.loc.gov/2020043603

2 4 6 8 10 9 7 5 3 1

New Directions Books are published for James Laughlin
by New Directions Publishing Corporation
80 Eighth Avenue, New York 10011

How to philosophize with a hammer...
Friedrich Nietzsche

Contents

Vladimír Boudník demonstrates "Explosionalism"
on the streets of Prague, c. 1955
Photo by Jaromír Pergler

Vladimír loved the outskirts of the city. He loved the dug-up streets, spilling their innards of pipes, conduits, and cables, all those black, distended shoots and tentacles that threatened to entangle terrified pedestrians like the snakes in the sculpture of Laocoön. Vladimír loved piles of freshly fired bricks and paving stones randomly tossed onto heaps of disgorged earth, the entrails of a big city laid bare, and he likened these torn-up streets to his own graphic art. He found creativity in disorder, and although he believed it prudent to repair those sewers and electrical conduits, all those pipes and connections, he also liked them just as they were, the trenches bridged with planks and hastily constructed walkways, the way they do it in the crypt of the Cathedral of St. Vitus whenever they uncover another rotunda, another chapel. Vladimír could never get enough of all that beauty, where chaos had an order of its own.

In writing down these memories of him I will use his methods; I too will leave the text exposed, like an excavated street, and it will be up to the readers, wherever it pleases them, to lay over the trench, full of fast-flowing, tossed-off sentences and words, a plank or makeshift gangway to carry them to the other side ... Dichtung und Wahrheit. Poetry and truth.

Bohumil Hrabal at the Embankment of Eternity, 1962

A Journal Written at Night

B ack then, when Vladimír returned home late at night from
work, from his marvelous meetings and encounters, he
would stretch out fully clothed on his bed in Libeň, at 24, Na
Hrázi Věčnosti, the Embankment of Eternity. He would ar-
range the adjustable lamp above his pillow and, bathed in a
cone of electric light, he would write letters to himself, his
journal. Back then, on autumn evenings, Vladimír would
write those entries in an enormous notebook like those used
in breweries to record the different batches of beer, or the
ledgers slaughterhouse managers use to keep track of the pur-
chase and sale of livestock. Vladimír wrote his daily accounts
not because he wanted to, but because he had to, because writing was part of his psychotherapy. The writing hand served as a
safety valve to the overheated furnace of his brain. Sometimes
he wrote his nocturnal diary with a carpenter's pencil. His
thoughts flowed so swiftly he could scarcely keep pace with
the images that possessed and consumed him. He was tied to
that notebook the way a telephone directory is chained to its

booth. He lacerated his diary with his carpenter's pencil, tormented by migraines that pounded nails into his head, and by a gallbladder that unlocked his liver with a red-hot key. But the more he wrote, the faster his illnesses and obsessions would fade. And when, several times a night, he would roar with victorious laughter, the last wrinkles would vanish from his brow, his maniacal powers would subside, and his working day would end, only to continue in other dimensions, in constellations of delirious visions and extravagant dreams.

Back then, a quarter of a century ago, when Vladimír would write in his journal at night, he often found himself caught in moral quandaries, and he would haltingly force his way, as through a narrow bottleneck, from brilliant imaginative associations to real material in motion. The anticipation and discovery of new artistic techniques would intensify his aggressiveness as he pushed himself out of a prolonged adolescence toward a manhood that had yet to come. Unable at the time to arrive in a single leap at a way of expressing the inner coherence of matter in his art, that is, to move directly from his own subjective, private perception of matter to generalities and objectivity, he suffered so acutely from hypochondria and hysteria that he'd push situations and experiences to the brink of brachial violence and personal insults. In the letters he wrote to his friends, he could be deliberately provocative, aiming not at reconciliation, not at a return to how things were, but at the synthesis of a grander identity that he would then, in his art, break apart again in order to reach a higher level of creative and human cognition.

Back then, a quarter of a century ago, when Vladimír wrote in his journal by night, I lived in the room next to his, in a former ironworker's shop, where I too was hunting and pecking my way to new realms of expression and understanding. Roughly speaking I was trying, through realism, to get beyond psychic automatism, to get back to writing about actual experiences and events. Vladimír and I would shout at each other from the doorways of our respective rooms, tearing our guts out and flinging them at each other. We'd yell at each other, not just through slammed doors but through walls and apartment blocks, from Žižkov to Libeň and back again, unaware that we were arguing at cross-purposes.

Back then, to be on the safe side, Vladimír would hide my hatchet and I, to be on the safe side, would lock up his kitchen knife. But anyone who thought we weren't fond of each other would have been wrong. Twenty-four hours after each psychic pogrom, we would once again be plying each other with beer and Vladimír would charm the regulars and invite those standing around the bar in their slippers, waiting to take jugs of beer home, to partake in the delights of his animated conversation. Afterward we'd walk through the outskirts of the city, gradually coming back to our constant preoccupation, the problems of art. We'd gaze down at Prague from Pražačka in Žižkov, and Šlosberk, the castle heights of Libeň, our eyes sparkling with reflections of the city lights at night. Later, in Vladimír's room, we would digest those vast, incomprehensible views of the metropolis garlanded in electric light by seeing it through Vladimír's microscope, which would send us into transports of delight by revealing the laws of motion within billion-faceted matter. And my hatchet would once more be standing in the hallway and Vladimír's kitchen knife would be resting innocently on his table.

Back then, when Vladimír would write in his journal at night, it was like the procedure in an operating room where they record the state of the patient's internal organs and, just as it reflected the way he lived with me at Number 24, Na Hrázi Věčnosti, the Embankment of Eternity, it also resembled the way in which he imposed his rhythmic oscillation of love and anger not only on his fellow students at art school, but on his own mother, his colleagues at work, and his bosses. The image that best captures the way he related to people is a sinusoid, a sine-wave oscillation, ebb and flow, black and white. He loved and terrorized everyone he met with such mad intensity because he would rather have seemed like a lunatic than a conventional bourgeois. The poet Egon Bondy* often came to see us, and whenever Vladimír read him something from his journal, Bondy would stamp the heels of his shoes on the floor and shout: "Goddamn it! I'd have to dig up an entire town square with my little finger to come up with an image like that! And they come tumbling out of his sleeve by the hundreds! Vladimír, for God's sake, write poems!" And Vladimír would laugh innocently, a lock of his hair would slip down over his forehead, and he'd beam with happiness, because at times, he was as open to emotion and praise as a child who's just seen his first candlelit Christmas tree.

If Vladimír was in a good mood, the moment we were out in the street he'd hike up his leg and plant the sole of his shoe on the top rung of the lamplighter's ladder chained to the light. In that position, Vladimír, who was almost six foot six, would tie his shoelace and Egon would walk under his leg and shout:

* The pen name of the philosopher and writer Zbyněk Fišer.

"Goddamn it! When I tell Zbyněk Fišer about this, he'll be thrilled!" And to beguile the passersby, Vladimír would stay that way, with his foot propped up against the streetlamp. The gaslight would illuminate his tousled hair and people would stop and stare at him in silence.

Back then, almost a quarter of a century ago, when Vladimír was writing his journal by night, he gathered a group of apprentices at the ČKD heavy engineering plant and taught them how easy it was to take random stains and spatters and blotches and turn them into recognizable images. Thus, what Vladimír had failed to achieve with his friends, which was to establish a clan, a community of like-minded artists, he managed to do with the apprentices. They'd go to the Chestnut Tree in Vysočany after work, and Vladimír would give his all to those young people. They could ask him anything and he'd lecture them exhaustively on his creative methods. He'd also write them letters with the same erudite precision as he once wrote to Professor Vondráček. When it was time for the apprentices to go home, Vladimír would turn his attention to the regulars who'd joined him at the table, and with the same patience and attention to detail he'd explain that while not everyone can be an artist, anyone can complete an image he sees in a crack in the wall.

Back then, when Vladimír was writing in his journal by night, a young carpenter, Mr. Kaifr, came to live with him, and when Mr. Kaifr returned from his shift, he'd gel and comb his hair, lie down on his bunk, and go straight to sleep. I'd often see Vladimír kneeling under his adjustable lamp – sunlight never penetrated our flat so we kept the lights on during the day – and Vladimír's curls would glisten in the lamplight and he'd talk about the miraculous qualities of matter and the impression it leaves in the human brain, but of course Mr. Kaifr would be sound asleep. Yet, after several months of mentoring in the principles of Explosionalism, Mr. Kaifr began working on a jewel case for his girlfriend, and he decorated the lid with twelve images he'd seen in the smoky patterns in the lacquered wood and then completed them with a brush.

Back then, when Vladimír was writing his journal at night, he invited Bouše, a friend, to stay with him. At the time, Bouše was working construction on a hydroelectric dam and he came home so exhausted that rather than working on his art, as Vladimír had hoped, he'd go straight to bed. So Vladimír brought in another friend, Pithart, a graphic artist who worked day and night on his lithographs, etching images into sheets of metal resting on an enormous slab of iron. At a different time each night the slab would crash off the table and not only shake the building, but rouse the entire street, and the tenants would get out of bed and run along the courtyard gallery in their nightclothes. Vladimír alone was amused, even delighted, by such unexpected awakenings, because he loved trouble and catastrophe. Vladimír even seemed to attract misfortune, and he treated things that would alarm or terrify others as a gift.

Back then, I'd often walk past his window and peer in, and my disbelief at what I saw in Vladimír's room would keep me awake at night, so I'd go back for another look, and I'd almost always see the same thing: Vladimír kneeling under his adjustable lamp, lecturing to the sleeping Kaifr and Bouše on the subject of Explosionalism, as if beseeching them to pay attention while rhythmically waving my hatchet over their heads. His two friends appeared to be listening to him, though the

messages were reaching them through different, somnoles-
cent realms of perception. Pithart was the only one actually at
work, creating large, realistic lithographs. Sometimes a beautiful woman in a leather coat would show up and bring Pithart
a bag of food, and then the only movement in the chiaroscuro
of the room came from the sharp hatchet blade and two tin
spoons, while the edges of the enormous iron slab glinted ominously, as if trying to decide on the right time to crash to
the floor. The beautiful woman in the leather coat was a clerk
in the police department, and she later persuaded Pithart to
move out, because he had lost a lot of weight working on those
lithographs. When they lugged the iron plate away, carrying
it between them like a sewing machine, the tenants and the
neighbors were relieved.

*

That was more or less how Vladimír lived when he was writing his journal at night. He was a creative, dogmatic disciple
of his own beliefs, a synthesis of Stavrogin and Prince Mysh-
kin, a master of horror and unfathomable humility, an artist
who, as the years went by, managed through the power of his
creativity to convert his negativity into something positive. He
would have been fifty this year and his friends, who feel his
presence as if he were still alive, are about to reissue a memo-
rial edition of his journal, using texts he had selected himself
from that enormous book, texts he considered important and
had self-published under his own imprint, Explosionalism Edi-
tions, and to which he gave the title One Seventh. It must be
added that Vladimír's death opened a window into his life, a
life in which he tried to penetrate the very structure and heart

of matter, to capture its inner beauty and, in his lithographs, to celebrate and breathe spirit into the mother of all matter.

*

Once Vladimír, the poet Marysko, and I set off to forage for wild mushrooms. On the train, we joked about the connection between Vladimír's recent wedding and the gold ring that glittered on his finger. Mr. Marysko had aesthetic objections to the ring. He thought it too conventional.

"You don't like the ring?" Vladimír asked.

The poet said he did not.

Vladimír pulled the ring off his finger and flung it out of the moving train into the rapidly receding forest of Klánovice. We raised our eyebrows, stunned into silence, because we knew how much Vladimír loved that ring, a symbol of his love for Tekla, the woman with whom he'd just exchanged vows. Then, with no emotion in his voice, Vladimír spoke to the silenced compartment about how and why tubercular cows produce the most milk.

Today I know that in Vladimír's mind, tossing the ring from the moving train in a single gallant gesture was a creative act, all the more so because of the pain its loss caused him. Vladimír dealt with everything the way he dealt with the ring, even his own life. Five years ago, on December 5, 1968, the eve of the day they celebrate Nicholas, the saint who, with great joy and love, gave away everything he had, Vladimír conducted an experiment on himself. He did not know, nor in his guilelessness could he have known, that the final link in the chain of causality was about to be broken. He believed the door handle would click deceptively, that the rope around his neck would tighten, and that a human hand, as it always had in the past, would arrive to help. But it did not, and Vladimír plunged headfirst from the embankment of the present into the heart of eternity.

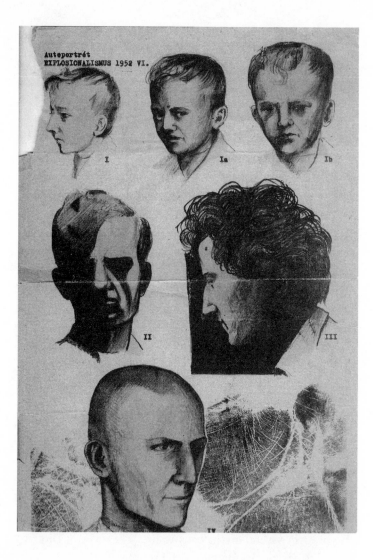

Self-portrait – Explosionalism
offset, 1952

The Gentle Barbarian

Vladimír, the master of tactile imagination, was always dying, always on the point of giving up the ghost, but only in order to rise from the dead, grow young again, renew the strength to break through walls with his head, to push through to the other side, to follow an umbilical cord back to the beginning of things, back to that first week when the world was created. At one and the same time, he could be both as ancient as the earth and as young as the dawn's first light, as leaves emerging from their buds. Vladimír was able to put his existence, constantly renewing, constantly aspiring toward youth, at risk. He could shake it up, subject it to trial by fire. That's why he loved pain. If the pain didn't come from without, he would inflict it upon himself. He felt responsible only to himself and to the elements of which he was composed. Through his graphic art he was able to give back to the elements ennobled versions of their material structure.

He brought several myths back to life. The myth of Dionysus, the handsome drunk who is the source of creativity, and the myth of Antaeus, the hero who could renew his waning strength only by touching the earth. Vladimír could be transported by the sight of a cement mixer and what was inside it, a vat of melting tar, a pneumatic drill, an acetylene torch purring quietly and glowing with a blue light, a coil of plumber's solder, a blowtorch, the frost encrusting a refrigerated display counter, the sight of a housepainter and the spattering of white paint on newspapers, dried flecks of sperm on jockey shorts, bloodstained sheets ...

All the vices of the age flowed through Vladimír: a fondness for mischief and playacting, pathological irritability, pet phobias, playing the fool and the imbecile, dogmatism, romantic melancholy and dreaminess, a hatred of neckties, a fondness for posters and banners (he loved being the flag bearer in parades), intolerance, contempt for intellectuals, humility, delusions of grandeur, a taste for obscenity, backyard gossip, hysteria, tetchiness, narcissism, sentimentality, paranoia.

Vladimír could do what a modern automobile engine can do: inject fuel directly into its cylinders, undiluted by air from the carburetor. Raw matter injected directly into the zone of transcendence. It required him to place great demands on the material he worked with. That Vladimír could do. The coefficient of pressures inside his head could withstand matter heated to the maximum degree, no more and no less so than Vincent van Gogh, Edvard Munch, Jackson Pollock. His emotions were what made him whole. That was the only way he could lay the foundations of scientific imagination. Only by relating subjectively to the matter he loved was he able to enter objectively into the spirit of the times. His lithographs are the apotheosis of a materialist worldview. Vladimír was a creative proletarian whose work celebrated human labor in a new way.

He joined forces with those who sought active ways of expressing their love for humanity, their desire to transform the world. He saw the social contract exclusively in terms of personal responsibility. By experimenting on himself, he was able to demonstrate that one can declare war only on oneself, that one can lay waste only to one's own territory, which is inside one's head. Through his life, he was able not only to show that the exploitation of man by man is a thing of the past but, in the name of creative Explosionalism, he was even able to nullify the class struggle, to show that it is possible to live in peace at the expense of the universe and oneself.

*

For Vladimír, the Carborundum grinders that threw up rooster tails of spark as they ground down the burrs and flaws on the steel ingots were a symbol of the power of education, both in individual lives and in society. For half a year, I worked on the shuttles in the Poldi steel mill, and when Vladimír would come into the workshop where there were ten grinding machines suspended from the ceiling on chains, operated by ten goggled grinder operators, he would be transfixed, staring at them unblinkingly, enthralled by what he was seeing and what his imagination was making of it.

*

Once Vladimír and I were walking home from Pudil's – or Kroft's, as the older regulars called it. Engrossed in an animated conversation, we passed an apparently abandoned baby carriage on the sidewalk with a child inside, crying. Vladimír stopped abruptly, analyzed the child's crying, and in two strides he was back at the carriage, reached inside, and removed a still-smoldering cigarette butt lying on the pillow next to the baby's head. He held it up theatrically and then ground it under his foot like a loathsome bug. Someone had tossed the remains of a burning cigarette out of a window. When we resumed our walk, he said, "Doctor, could I persuade you to buy me some paper and paints? If you will, here's what I'll do. Inspired by the baby in the buggy and the burning cigarette, I'll make an engraving, a great engraving, just for you, about that child. But you won't buy me either paints or paper. Or will you?"

*

Vladimír, Bondy, and I were so fond of beer that as soon as the first glasses were brought to our table, we'd shock everyone in the pub by dipping our hands into the foam, smearing our faces with it, rubbing it in our hair, as Jews rub sugar water into their *peyot*. When the second round arrived we'd smear ourselves with foam again, and we would turn all shiny and you could smell us a mile away. But we were just fooling around, showing off our love of beer and our youthful enthusiasm.

We were barons of the beer hall.

*

Vladimír was a fast walker and enjoyed moving swiftly around Prague. He'd take shortcuts between Žižkov and Libeň, Košiře and Střešovice. The afternoon he threw his wedding ring out the train window into the forest of Klánovice, he walked so quickly through the woods of Kersko that he lost us. Next morning, when I opened the door of my flat in Libeň, a note fell out that said: "Got back to Prague at midnight via Český Brod. Tell you about it later. Greetings, Vladimír."

He'd show up in Hlubočepy, or he'd suddenly drop in on his Surrealist friends in Mednik Hill. If he had an exhibition somewhere, he'd arrive the night before so he could savor every detail of the show and then, during the exhibition, he'd revel as much in what did not happen as in what did.

*

Vladimír was interested in things that might have happened. A friend of his had a collection of sandstone fossils weighing several hundred kilograms, and Vladimír taught him to draw in the Explosionalist manner, to incorporate impressions of those crustaceans into his portraits of people. But when that same friend invited him along to make fossil rubbings directly in the Koněprusy Caves, Vladimír refused to go. "Certainly not!" he said. "I've initiated you into the mysteries of active graphics. I've told you more than I've told anyone else, and now I'm worried. You know those caves well. You'll bump into me and knock me into a crevasse and then you'll pass off my ideas as your own. That's not going to happen. You can go there by yourself."

*

Vladimír hated money. The moment he got an advance, he'd spend it. Each day he'd run up debts, ten crowns here, twenty crowns there, then he'd carefully write the name of the creditors on his locker door, and settle up with them the moment he got his next pay packet. He'd give everyone what he owed them, then he'd stand there with what was left of the money in his hand, and laughing, he'd say: "What should I do with this? Toss it in the stove? Or spend it?" And he'd blow the rest the same night and then, with obvious relish, he'd cadge sixty hellers for carfare or cigarettes, and then go home on foot. When he earned several thousand crowns for illustrating a book, he was terrified. He gave two thousand to his mother, another two thousand to his mother-in-law, spent a few hundred right away, and then when his mother, convinced that Vladimír was flush, moved back home so he could enjoy the place without her, he blew the rest of the money in a maniacal spree and then, greatly relieved, borrowed sixty hellers for carfare home. Back then, we too thought that Vladimír would be financially okay for a few weeks. When I paid him a visit, a neighbor of his let me in and when I remarked that Vladimír now had enough money to tide him over for a while, she said: "That's where you're wrong. Last night he ate all the potatoes I'd left in the corridor to cool."

*

Back then, when we argued so vociferously because we had a reason to argue, the neighbors would blame the commotion on Vladimír, who objected: "Me? No, it was him!" and he'd point to my window, and when they'd blame it on me, I'd say: "Me? No, it was him!" and I'd point to Vladimír's window.

Eventually, our arguments came to a head. At the time, each of us was sleeping in his own room, Vladimír with my hatchet in bed with him and I with Vladimír's kitchen knife, and whenever one of us so much as moved, the other would move too, and when one of us got up, the other got up too. We'd turn on the light and, through the door connecting our rooms, we'd confirm that each had the other's weapon. So we decided to wall up the door. An elderly mason from Bratrská Street came over, we took the door off its hinges, the bricklayer put tar paper under the doorframe, and we signed a release with the landlady, promising to restore everything to its original condition when we moved out. The mason mixed his mortar in a barrow and began closing off the doorway as Vladimír and I sat, each at his own table, excited to see the bricks gradually mounting to form a barrier between us. It was like watching water rise, and soon we could see only the upper parts of our bodies, though Vladimír, because he was tall, was still seated. Next, all I could see was his head, then we got to our feet and the bricklayer stood between us on the overturned hod while we handed him the bricks that would divide us, like the old woman who carried her own bundle of straw to the fire that consumed Jan Hus at the stake. Finally, we could no longer see each other, but we zealously tried to outdo each other in the final phase, passing bricks to the mason who, by guesswork now, was layering his mortar in so the final bricks would neatly close the gap. When the mortar had dried we leaned the door back in its place, relieved to be shut off from each other at last.

When the bricks were still only waist high, Egon Bondy showed up and he ran back and forth along the hallway, first to my room, then to Vladimír's and, cupping his chin in his hand, he tried to make sense of this act of separation, since we could still reach each other's room through the corridor. "What the hell are you up to?" he cried in his high voice, then ran out into the courtyard, where the sun was pouring down hecto-liters of light beer, and whenever Egon stood in the sun he looked like a faun emerging from a brewery vat, his light-brown hair trickling down alongside his ears and his beard suffused with golden lager, and now he stood there shaking his fists and shouting: "Panie Wladimirze! Isn't it enough that Europe is cut off from itself by a wall, that Korea is cut off from itself, that a divided Berlin is cut off from itself? It doesn't mean a fart in the wind to you, does it!" And he stomped back inside and studied Vladimír's head from my vantage point, then ran round and looked at my head from Vladimír's side, savoring the moment, just as we would when the last brick, the last trowelful of mortar, had been set in place and we could no longer see each other.

That evening, when Vladimír came home and began writing in his journal, I could hear his pen moving energetically across the pages of his ledger more clearly than when there hadn't been that wall between us. And when Vladimír rolled over in bed, it was as though he'd rolled over right next to me. I could hear every breath he took, I could even hear his lungs expanding and his liver working and his heart beating more resoundingly than when there'd been no wall between us. We were polite to each other in the hallway, and back in our own private dens, we would savor the presence on the other side of the wall more intensely than ever before.

I moved my bed against the wall and the next day, from the courtyard, I could see that Vladimír too had shifted his bed against the wall, so we slept together like Siamese twins, attached by the spine of the wall that conjoined us far more firmly than when the door swung at will on its hinges.

"Are you asleep?" Vladimír would whisper.

"Not yet," I'd whisper to the wall.

"Me neither," Vladimír would whisper back.

Sometimes we didn't talk to each other at all, but it was enough for me to touch the wall with my finger and from the other side I could hear Vladimír sketching something in the plaster with his fingernail, our way of letting each other know that we were better friends now than ever before.

After Vladimír moved to Žižkov, he would drop around for a visit now and then, or I would meet him in a pub, and at the Bus Stop, a pub opposite the factory, we started arguing again. Once more, we became friends for life and unto death, but we no longer shouted at each other, now that each of us had found his own way and was no longer competing with the other, and Vladimír pulled his chair to the wall, I did the same with a kitchen stool on the other side, and we chipped away at the mortar with a chisel and with mounting excitement we loosened one brick, then another. It was as if we were operating on each other, cutting each other's chest open. We were astonished at how lovely the other's room looked, even though through the narrow opening we saw scarcely more than the forehead or the chin of the other and in the background, the sad, white wall. When we removed several more bricks we could each see the other's torso. Vladimír set an unfinished bottle of *griotka* on the wall, and from my side I topped the bottle off with rum, and we shook it and poured the mixture into a pair of glasses. As we were drinking a toast, Egon Bondy showed up and was astonished at what he saw. He got up on the stool and looked into Vladimír's room, then ran into the hall and into Vladimír's room and from there he looked at me, and at the wall in the doorway, which was now serving as a tabletop. I brought a small glass and filled it with the concoction. Egon took a drink and spat it out as though he'd taken a sip of acid. He stood facing the wall and pounded the plaster with both fists, bumped his forehead gently against the wall, then did the same on Vladimír's side and shouted: "Damn it all! It's détente! Mutual understanding among nations has broken out here and now! I'm going to consult the Zbyněk Fišer about this. It is a rose, it's not a rose, therefore it's a rose! A caress must be preceded by a slap in the face."

*

Vladimír liked to go about bareheaded. In inclement weather, he wore a black rabbi's hat cocked at a dandyish, Beau Brummellesque angle, and when the cold weather came, he sewed himself a fantastic fur cap from his mother's muff, the kind in fashion now, with a prominent peak, as the rebbes used to wear in Nikolsburg. On the rare occasions when he wore a necktie, it did not, at first glance, look like a tie, but more like a dog collar, and not a dog collar either, more like a piece of twine that he deliberately jinked to the left, so the knot was half-hidden by his shirt collar. He dreamed of owning an elegant cardigan with an elegant suit, but when the dream came true, he pronounced himself a moron, an imbecile, a fool ...

*

We loved drinking beer in the World Cafeteria in Libeň and watching the cleaning ladies at work. One of them, a former operetta singer, was now a septuagenarian who wore a lot of makeup and a flouncy apron. When she swept the floor, she would dance with the broom, and every man would gently kiss her hand when she turned to face him. Ever the soubrette, she would laugh, take sips of customers' beer, and when she wheeled away the service cart stacked with dirty dishes and leftovers, she sang gay little ditties. She was a crazy little spitfire, easy enough to laugh at. "Be careful," Vladimír cautioned. "She's a saint."

The second cleaning lady, also long since a pensioner, used to act in tragedies in amateur theater companies, her face a jaundiced, tragic mask worn down by the carnival of life. She would sigh as she swept, as if raking her own remains out of a crematorium oven. When she trundled away the service cart full of dirty dishes, she was carrying her bones to the scrapyard. A tragic case of bad conscience. "Careful!" Vladimír said. "She loves to drink, and she'll drink anything. She's already blown her pension on buckets of beer that she fills up at Vanista's. Another saint!"

We stood there, drinking our beers and watching the two saints, and each time a customer came in, the door would close automatically, slowly at first, then with a loud clatter, like an upright metal coffin clanging shut. Suddenly Egon Bondy walked in. "Where have you been?" he shouted. "I've been round half a dozen pubs looking for you," and he raised his arms in the doorway, and behind him, the door slammed shut with a deafening crash.

"Does it always do that?" Egon said, putting his fingers in his ears.

"No," Vladimír said, "only when someone comes in. Mrs. Vlaštovková, have you got a screwdriver?"

Vladimír pulled a chair up to the door, climbed on it, put on his glasses, tightened a screw on the door closer, and returned the screwdriver. We all waited for the next customer to come in. This time, the door closed gently, and only the cleaning lady jerked to attention, as though she'd had a needle stuck in her spine. Egon Bondy drank one beer after another and kept looking around, as though he expected something was about to happen. "What are you doing here anyway?" he asked.

"We're hunters on the lookout for game," Vladimír said.

Egon Bondy let the beer trickle into his beard, and while he was waiting for another glass, he sucked at his whiskers. An ambulance roared down from Primatorská Street, siren blaring, the blue light on its roof flashing. The tragic cleaning lady clapped her hand to her heart as the ambulance swerved to a halt in front of the World so abruptly it almost toppled over. Two old women in the passageway clutched their throats and cried out: "My God! Who is it this time?"

Egon Bondy blanched and fumbled for his pulse: "There's nothing wrong with me, damn it!"

Two attendants jumped out of the ambulance, pulled out a white oilcloth stretcher, each took two large jugs, hurried into the taproom, ordered Pilsner on tap, each drank a beer for the road, then polished off what was left in the glasses Mrs. Vlaštovková had used to fill the jugs. In the passageway the two old ladies were wiping each other's face with a handkerchief. The attendants rushed out with the jugs of beer, their white frock coats flapping behind them, slid the oilcloth stretcher with the jugs back into the ambulance, jumped into the cab, and drove off, siren blaring and lights flashing. It took the corner so fast it almost capsized, and people walking down from the Libeň Chateau across the street stopped with their hands on their hearts and wondered who it was they were taking away.

Egon Bondy said: "Holy shit! Some memento mori that is! Vladimír, how did you manage to conjure those idiots up?"

Vladimír was thrilled, while Egon's attention turned to a Zündapp that had just pulled up in front of the cinema, driven by a man in motorcycle leathers and a helmet as big and grim as a deep-sea diver's helmet. He dismounted and strode gravely into the passageway and then into the movie theater.

"What in God's name was that?" Egon sputtered.

"That's his job," Vladimír said. "He delivers the newsreel to the movie houses."

We watched as the helmeted motorcyclist emerged from the cinema, kick-started the Zündapp, and roared off to deliver the newsreel to a cinema where the feature started a half an hour later. We went on drinking. When we finally emerged in front of the Chateau, the streetlights above the tram stop had already come on, the Number 13 had pulled up, and a woman with a baby carriage was waiting to get into the last car. Someone helped her up but the driver closed the door prematurely with the woman still holding her end of the carriage, now trapped in the door. The tram began to move and the woman, gripping the handle, ran awkwardly after it, yelling at the driver, but the tram kept accelerating and the baby carriage struck a lamppost and snapped in two and people waiting for the next tram were screaming. A few of the braver ones ran up to the carriage. Egon turned white ... but then bottles of beer tumbled out of the broken baby carriage and smashed on the pavement and the smell of beer drifted down the street. The woman screamed after the departing streetcar: "There goes twenty bottles of beer! You'll pay for it, you bastards!" And then, pointing to

Vladimír and Egon, she said, "Gentlemen, you saw it all. Will you be my witnesses?"

"Bottles of beer?" Egon Bondy shouted. "Bottles of beer? What about the baby? I heard bones cracking!"

And the woman said, "That was the beer case. You don't expect an old lady to carry twenty bottles of beer in her bare hands, do you?"

Vladimír beamed with excitement. Egon Bondy staggered into the darkness of the park, waving his arms as if trying to shake off a bad dream. "Holy shit! What a gag! Not even Chaplin could have come up with that one."

*

If someone were pushing a loaded wagon along the street, Vladimír would be there to help, not so much out of love for his neighbor as for the feel of his hands on the bar. If someone were unloading coal, Vladimír would ask if he could help. And again, not even a lover with his hand on a loved one's thighs was happier than Vladimír shoveling coal, reveling in the sensation of his hands on the haft, on the slippery bucket handle. He never tried to avoid coal dust or soot, on the contrary, when he was done, he would leave the dark, dusty smears under his nostrils.

*

Once, we went for a walk along Pod Koráb and were astonished to see that the hillside, once neglected and bare, was now divided into geometric plots, future gardens and allotments, and people were already pulling up weeds and turning the soil over with spades. The more ambitious ones worked at night as well and had already planted strawberries and vegetables. Vladimír would choose a plot where the least amount of work had been done and offer to help out, battling the weeds, throwing his whole body into it. He loved talking about how, when he turned over the soil, he would have the tactile sensation of deflowering the virgin Earth with his spade.

Back then we helped a woman who would bring her baby with her in a stroller, and the baby would cry, because the heat of the sun on that hillside was so intense. Vladimír would let his light-brown curls tumble into the sunlight, and the woman would run to her child and sometimes take out her breast and give the baby a drink ... Toward evening, when Vladimír would take his leave and promise to come again the next day, the woman, perhaps thinking that Christ was walking the earth again, would kiss the back of his hand ...

Another time, when Vladimír was helping a pensioner pile coal in the woodshed in the courtyard and talking to her about his problems and his work, the old woman became more and more agitated, staring at the axe embedded in the chopping block. In desperation, she covered the axe with her apron, then heaved a sigh of relief when Vladimír and I left, hurrying into the street to see if we'd really gone to Hausman's, as we'd said ...

*

Vladimír made cream from skim milk, diamonds from coal dust, a phoenix from a sparrow, and he could turn a cripple into a contender. Whenever there was too little of something, he'd rush in with his talent to show that *omnia ubique* – everything is everywhere – and that the maximum resided in the minimum, that every point in the world was the center of a

Garden of Eden, whereas all hanging gardens eventually become ruins and dust and in that dust all beauty persists, and in that tiny fragment of earth, everything begins anew ...

*

In the Old Post Office, where a pretty, plump young Gypsy girl slung the beer, Vladimír liked to sit in the taproom and write letters. As always, he attracted real characters. When I sat down at his table, a good-looking young man was talking to him: "I first met her when my arm was in a cast," the man was saying, "and that was the arm I'd put around her neck and she'd always groan, but she got used to it. The boys would draw all kinds of things on the cast, and there was this one writer who came to give a talk at the hospital, and I didn't have one of his books so he signed the cast instead. But now comes the ugly part. They take the cast off and my girl, though we'd already agreed to get married, tells me I'm not as gentle to her as I used to be, and she up and leaves me. And then yesterday, you could've knocked me over! Who do I see? My old girlfriend, stepping out with this guy who has his arm, the same one as mine, in a cast. These girls are all depraved."

Vladimír kept on writing, but spoke in a voice hoarse with outrage: "Mine left me too, so I'm writing the prosecutor. The presiding judge advised me to go easy on her, so I'm writing her love letters. This is my sixth. But look here, my friend, do you know what Martonová's experiments are? Martonová's a doctor. I'm one of her guinea pigs right now. You take your clothes off. They show you a movie with lots of nudity. I'm all wired up, and there's some kind of apparatus attached to my cock. A pornographic film. The little lights on the machine are winking away, the needles flying back and forth, drawing squiggly lines, information for the shrinks to process. On top of everything else, the machines revealed the old Oedipal thing. You know? When mother gets up in the morning, I'm there waiting for her. I walk around naked, make it look like an innocent blunder. She still has a fabulous little body. She pretends she doesn't see me."

The young man was looking thoughtful, resting his chin in his hands, fingertips close to his eyes. Then he said, carefully: "The bill, please. You know, that girl probably takes after her dad. He's from up north, in the Giant Mountains, and one time he takes his driver's license and his ID book and goes into the municipal office and tells them to change his employment status 'cause he's got a new job: "Anton Hulík – God." A month later they pick him up at the train station in the freezing cold with nothing on but a tee shirt. In the asylum, they didn't give him shock treatments, they gave him so-called pukecillin, and after the injections he barfed so much that in three months, he was skin and bones. Five months later, he's just a normal guy again, a plumber, and they gave him back his driver's license and his ID book." The young man got up, ceremonially rapped his knuckles on the tablecloth, and walked out.

Vladimír went on writing furiously, little rivulets of red dessert wine glistening in the corners of his mouth, and the bartender was bringing him what was certainly his third large glassful, and what a letter this was going to be! What a letter, Lord have mercy, the fourth page and Vladimír still hasn't come down the hill, but keeps climbing higher, still in that maniacal mood in which he'll say things he'll regret tomorrow.

I left Vladimír to his writing and went for a walk around the Libeň Chateau, where I ran into my former doctor, a retired general practitioner. He was standing with his arm extended, palm upward, trying to attract titmice to come and eat peanuts from his hand. When he saw me, he said: "Ah, you're looking better now, not ready for a postmortem just yet... My my my! So, have you changed your reading habits? Something lighthearted, maybe? A humor magazine, perhaps? Yesterday, a rabbit got caught in a snare here and strangled. Where in the world is my little crested tit, my little blue tit? So, is it still suppurating, still suppurating? That's good. And what about your stool? Back to normal? It is? Well, that's just wonderful. Chalk up another one for science."

I turned so the doctor could get a better look at me. He peered at me and then, in the same tone of voice, said: "Children also try to get birds to eat from their hand, but sometimes they try to catch them. There's no trusting children. But you know that bottle of kirsch you gave me? My wife and I drank it under the Christmas tree, finished it off at one go. Oh, dear me! Where's my little blue tit, my nuthatch? What time is it? Of course, those little hooligans strangled the rabbit we've been feeding here for ten years." He leaned in close, grasped my arm in his bony fingers and whispered: "You should not be flirting with suicide ..."

"But that's not me. It's Vladimír you're thinking of!" I said.

And he said, in these exact words: "But you are Vladimír ... Oh, dear me! Where's my little blue tit today? My nuthatch? Dear me ..."

*

Vladimír was persuaded by friends to go with them into the countryside, into the world of appearances, to find subjects to paint. Two days later he came back with his easel and box of paints, but no paintings. He seemed overwhelmed, exhausted from lack of sleep, dazed. "Doctor, I'm done with nature! We were painting a small stand of trees near Kladno, a modest little landscape, and just as we were putting on the final touches, the police showed up and arrested us for spying. They grilled us all night about who was paying us to do the painting, because it turns out that with a little imagination, beyond that stand of trees, beyond those bright tree trunks, you can see the Kladno steel mills, and if our paintings were to fall into enemy hands they'd know their exact location. Just beyond those woods. And that made us spies. Doctor, I'd rather carry on painting with only the universe to answer to. I'd rather be a spy on behalf of the heavens!"

About a year later, Rotbauer persuaded Vladimír to go painting with him on the outskirts of Prague. And so, from the Libeň bridge, they painted one of the inlets of the Vltava. That same afternoon Egon Bondy came to the Embankment of Eternity looking for Vladimír. He wanted the three of us to go for a walk up the Rokytka creek and, as evening fell, we'd find a place to sit, drink, and sing folk songs, like Vladimír's favorite, "The Falcon in the Maple." I told him where Vladimír was likely to be, and we set off to meet him. And there he was. I could see Vladimír's head high above the crowds walking along the main street, but he was not alone. He and Rotbauer were accompanied by policemen while an old pensioner hopped along behind them shouting: "Good people. These men are subversives. Spies." And Vladimír was smiling, holding his box of paints, while the policemen carried both canvases. We followed them to Božena Němcová Street, and on to Rosenberg Street. Then we waited for them.

Three hours later, drinking Pilsner in the World Cafeteria, we saw Vladimír and Rotbauer walk out of the police station. Over beer, Vladimír explained: "The pensioner called the police. He claimed there's a boatyard of strategic importance to the state just past the inlet we were painting. We tried to explain that we were only interested in painting trees, but they brought us in anyway, and we had to make a sworn statement. I think we're going to have to stick to humanist abstraction."

Egon Bondy cursed and swore. "Jesus, Vladimír! You've got more luck than brains. The secret police are coming and going through my door all the time, but no one knows about it. And they parade you back through the streets full of people. Goddamn it! All that glory! I'm jealous!"

*

Vladimír liked to take long streetcar rides, waiting for the moment when the conductor up front would punch several dozen tickets at once with her ticket punch. He'd close his eyes, place his hand on his gallbladder and experience different layers and phases of reality at once. First he'd have a tactile sensation of being that book of streetcar tickets as they were being punched, then he'd experience a gallbladder attack that felt as though the conductor was puncturing his liver, and finally he experienced the perforation of his duodenum. When he opened his eyes again, he'd go for a walk and think of how he would punch holes in his lithographs, to replicate the physical sensation he'd experienced on the tram.

That was what Vladimír's sensibility was like. He liked to talk about how terrified he was of the moment the tailor who was fitting him for a new suit would kneel in front of him and gently, discreetly, insert his fingers between his legs to secure the tape as he measured the length of his inseam ... and how, in that ritual moment, he would faint. Whenever there was a plane crash, Vladimír wanted to know all the details. He would experience the catastrophe as a passenger catapulted into the air or burned up as the plane fell to earth, or struck by shards of metal as the engines exploded. It was as though he became the aircraft itself as it plunged into the ocean or plummeted to earth or was blown to bits in midair and then fell in fragments to the landscape below. When he learned that the insurance companies, to determine the cause of the crash, would gather up the debris and reassemble it into a replica of the original aircraft, Vladimír was thrilled. "That's just like me! That's exactly how I put myself back together again once a week."

*

Vladimír was capable of working himself up into a state of rabid morbidity, only to blow it up in his graphic art. There was a rhythm to it. He was either too sick or too healthy, and the state he happened to be in was exactly how he appeared to anyone who met him. But nature proceeds like Vladimír, because nature existed before he did. You might even say that Vladimír was nature's student, her product, her admirer ...

Once Vladimír and I set off for the Brdy forest to hunt for wild mushrooms. But mushrooms were not the point of our journey. We wanted to travel along the section of track where Egon Bondy had lain down one night, drowsy with opiates, to get himself painlessly run over. But that night, the track where he lay down had been taken out of service and he woke up the next morning, not in the kingdom of ontology, but still lying on the rails, while the trains roared by on the other line.

We got to the Smíchov train station with time to spare so we walked along the platform, admiring the locomotives. An engineer was wiping down a condenser and I went up to him and said: "Mr. Kopič, if they were to shoot you a low pass right up the middle, could you still dribble through your opponents and score a goal?"

Mr. Kopič, a former center forward for the Polaban Nymburk soccer club, replied proudly: "You bet I could! And you know, I still like kicking the old ball around. Do I know you?"

"I'm a fan of yours from Nymburk, from the brewery," I said.

And while Vladimír looked on in amazement, Mr. Kopič said: "Gentlemen, it's just about departure time. May I have the pleasure?" And he made a sweeping, courtly gesture, inviting us aboard the locomotive.

We climbed into the cabin and Mr. Kopič waited for the signal from the dispatcher, then he pulled the throttle and eased the train out of the station. Once we were underway, Mr. Kopič told us how, just outside of Smíchov, a man had dragged his son onto the tracks and got them both run over. He'd seen the son struggling to escape, but the father was stronger, like Abraham when he was about to sacrifice his son, Isaac, except that God reprieved Abraham at the last minute, whereas the easygoing Mr. Kopič, though he applied the brakes, ran over the father and son, and all he saw was their legs flopping about . . .

The tale moved Vladimír to tears. When the cloud of misfortune had lifted, Vladimír asked if he could hold the throttle. Mr. Kopič said he could. Vladimír gripped the lever and looked out the window for a while, then he handed it over and declared: "Just by touching that lever, you can feel the whole locomotive, the whole train, the whole track!"

"This is the spot where Egon Bondy lay down on the rail line," I said, pointing to it, and Vladimír declared: "What we experienced in those few minutes is Apollinaire's Zone!" And he stood there ecstatically, his legs apart. And I, who have often traveled by train and savored the vibrations of the locomotive, the click-clack each time the wheels passed over a joint in the tracks, I registered all of it with my whole body, because I was a dispatcher during the war. I also worked with track maintenance crews, and my job was to ride along in the cab and determine, by sensing the movement of the engine, whether there were any problems with the switches and report on any repairs to the roadbed that needed doing.

I knew that Vladimír was experiencing the train in motion as a direct, tactile sensation. Once again, his eyes were wide open and I knew that, in that precise moment, Vladimír had become the train, the locomotive, and the entire rail line. And as the coupling between the engine and the tender jerked back and forth, gently, brutally, suggesting a kind of sexual communion between them, Vladimír leaned toward me and whispered: "I've got the most amazing erection!" The train stopped in Zadní Třebaň. Mr. Kopič wiped his hands with detergent oil and as he was saying goodbye to us, he apologized for the grime. "You know, Vojta Hulík's engine was so clean he'd wear white gloves to operate it."

*

When Vladimír was in the throes of creation, he usually worked in the nude. He loved being naked, and he would approach the silk screen or the copper plate as though it were a kind of fore-play. He'd gradually work himself up into a state of erotic and therefore creative excitement, timing it so that between the etching and the distressing of the plates a beautiful arc would bend, stretching between erection and ejaculation. When he worked with a silk screen, he would rub the paper with his semen. All his graphic works were covered with a gentle layer of sexual viscosity.

*

Once Vladimír and I set off for Mělník to drink the local Ludmila wine. In the crypt of the cathedral, Vladimír admired the ossuary and in particular two skulls eaten away by syphilis. Vladimír also loved the confluence of the Vltava and the Labe rivers, because the Vltava was mightier than the Labe, and this pleased him, and he loved to point out that although from Mělník on, the river was called the Labe, and then in Germany, the Elbe, it should by rights be called the Vltava all the way to the sea. Then we went on foot all the way to Beřkovice, where we walked around the wall surrounding the insane asylum until evening. Vladimír was so taken with that institution that he said he wanted to live there one day. Next we set off for Liběchov, and though it was already dark, Vladimír found a headless statue under a bushy tree by the stream, reminding us of a headless statue near the Rokytka creek in Libeň. Then we washed away the taste of the Ludmila wine with beer, and that night, following the Stations of the Cross, we walked up a path that led to a derelict church.

The moon was full and from the deep shadows cast by the

trees lining the road, we emerged into limelight. At the top of the hill, by the little church, it was unpleasantly windy so we lay down in a sheltered spot and looked out at the countryside. The asylum in Beřkovice shone brilliantly in the moonlight. Then Vladimír felt for the church door and opened it gently and we entered the ruined building. Shafts of moonlight streamed in through a chink in the wall. Three pilgrimage banners furled in their sleeves stood by the pews. Vladimír arranged a kind of bed on the altar and lay down. He put a brick under his head. I lay down beside him, but I had nothing to support my head, so Vladimír gave me his brick and then tucked his elbow under his head. The moonlight pouring into the chapel was dazzling. Vladimír climbed down and brought back one of the banners and we covered ourselves with it. He stretched out his leg and with the tip of his shoe, touched the altar lamp, its eternal flame long extinguished, and set the ornate vessel, suspended on three copper chains linked to a single chain attached to the ceiling, swinging so that it arced into the chlorine light of the moon and burst into flame. Each time, the pendulum of eternity would disappear into the darkness like a nocturnal bird, but when it reappeared in the moonlight, the vessel was on fire like a magnificent pheasant, like the Phoenix. For an instant it would hang motionless at the top of its arc, and then, through gravity and the easy movement of Vladimír's shoe, it would swing back again into the darkness. The entire mechanism creaked gently as the links rubbed against each other like the discs in an ailing spine. Vladimír's eyes were open all night, staring at the swinging, eternal flame, unblinking. We lay there on our backs like Přemyslid kings with their wives.

By dawn, Vladimír had fallen asleep with a beatific smile on his face and the pilgrimage banner over his chest. As it grew lighter, I could see that he was covered with the torso of St. Wenceslas, and that the saint's legs, embroidered in silver and gold thread, were covering me. Wenceslas, who loved to drink and talk to animals, was stabbed to death by his own brother, for no matter where you are in the world, you will never be forgiven for desiring a life of peace, in thrall to inebriation and therefore to the universe.

*

For Vladimír, agony and ecstasy were a single door through which one entered and exited, because going through that door meant death and coming out again meant life. Instead of turning things inside out Vladimír turned them outside in. For him, to be born was to die, and to die was to be born. That is why he was prone to stigmata. His hands and feet were covered with scars, but it was not to honor Christ's open wounds; his stigmata came from working with metal and from the other techniques of the black art of smithing. He was so in love with his factory that had he raised the bar of his hysteria any higher, copper filings would pour out of his fingers, he would cough up metal chips, and spit out steel dust ... When iron and sulphur, magnesium and carbon, calcium and water, and all the other minerals and metals that nature assembles to make a human body, when they came near Vladimír's body, the same elements within him would become excited and call out and Vladimír's only recourse was to heed their longing and their love for those fellow metals and minerals that, when the body dies, rise again from the dead to circulate once more in the kingdom of metamorphoses ...

*

When I returned from a trip to Paris, I debriefed Vladimír for several hours about what I'd seen. Vladimír was thrilled. "From what you say, Doctor, Paris must be magnificent, almost like Libeň, and maybe even like Vysočany. And when I let my fantasy run free, Paris is as beautiful as Žižkov. What you've just told me has made me fall in love again with Utrillo, with his walls, those cracked walls he painted so beautifully that the moment you see them you want to pull out your pecker and piss against them. As I say, Doctor, Paris must be magnificent ..."

*

Vladimír approached everything ritually, sacramentally. He always showed up at work half an hour early so he could take his time getting dressed, the way a priest would don his robes before serving mass. When a letter came in the mail, at first he could scarcely believe it. He'd come back from the postbox, carefully checking and double-checking the address. When he was finally satisfied that it was really addressed to him, he'd place the letter on the table, carefully wash his hands, and then, even more carefully, open it. He'd walk around the room, sit down, put on his glasses, and slowly read it, then fold it, then read it again, then put the letter away in a case, along with hundreds of other letters and thousands of other pieces of writing.

In the same way, when he wrote, he wouldn't just approach the task casually. First he'd make an entry in his journal, and then he'd retire to somewhere secluded, his favorite spot being a pub, where he'd order a beer and a glass of *hořčák*, a bittersweet fruit wine, and if he wanted the letter to be exceptionally audacious, he'd have another glass of the wine. And when at last he felt himself in a state of grace, he'd start to write and the words would gush from his pen as from a water main turned on full. When he'd finished writing, he'd light a ceremonial cigarette and consider what kind of response the letter might evoke. If he felt it might provoke outrage, he'd order another glass of the bittersweet wine to give him the gumption to seal the letter and toss it in the mailbox. He'd always drum on the box and poke his fingers into the slot to see if the letter could be retrieved. The next day he'd wonder if the letter had arrived and in his mind he'd savor, through the recipient's eyes and mind, the outrage, the pain, or sometimes even the pleasure his letter might have caused. Vladimír's letters were always personal and always aggressive. The more he thought his letter might hurt the addressee, the more invigorated he felt.

Whenever Vladimír went somewhere on a visit, he'd take the whole afternoon to get ready. He'd carefully bathe, shave, and check in the mirror to see which suit or sweater looked best on him. When he was climbing the stairs or entering the house he was visiting, he'd be faint with anticipation and worried to death about what to say. No matter whom he was going to meet, he'd always prepare for the encounter as though he were going to meet a girl before whom he might have to undress.

He approached his art in the same way. His preparation was always impeccable, whether he was wearing clothing he had carefully selected, or was naked. His work with the silk screen was always like the celebration of a mass, a ministration, an academic procession. Catholic ritual had seeped into Vladimír's subconscious, which is why no matter what event he was taking part in, his actions always took on the aspect of a ritual mystery. Ceremony, however, allowed Vladimír, in any company, not only to say what he had against it and its individual members, but to attack them in such a way that the targets of his frankness would be thrown off balance. Vladimír's sense of ceremony was a mask that allowed him to confess, in all decency, his complexes, his obscene sexual and erotic fantasies. Vladimír could enthrall people the way a python can hypnotize a rabbit. At first he'd completely agree with everyone in the room, and allow that each was right, then he'd pounce, and say: "If you'll permit me ..." and he'd reverse his previous statement and, as in a mass, he'd transubstantiate an ordinary wafer and goblet of wine into his own body and his own blood and anoint those present with it, whether they wanted it or not.

*

Vladimír wasn't fond of dialogue. Or he was, but only on his own terms. Proper dialectics he understood exclusively as an argument with himself, as a way of forcing the contending opposites within him into monologue. Monologue was Vladimír's cup of tea ...

*

Not only was Vladimír drawn to the crime reports and local news in all the evening papers, he was always able to rise above events, even those he experienced with deadly intensity. Once we set off for Klánovice, and as we were walking past cottages and villas, Vladimír's attention was drawn to a tall pine tree with a chain wrapped around its trunk. Some cottagers were cutting it down and trying to force it to fall between a cottage and a garage. An arboreal tragedy was about to happen, for the tree was going to be brought screaming to the ground by a saw and axes. A winch, the kind used in marinas to pull boats into the jetty, was attached to the trunk, and Vladimír stared in alarm as a worker pumped the lever and brought the hundred-year-old tree to the point where it began to topple. But to everyone's horror, the crown started twisting to one side and the tree was now angled to fall directly onto the garage, threatening to flatten it to the ground. "Oh, my God!" cried the workers, petrified. And it was Vladimír who leaped into action, gave the handle of the winch several pumps, forcing the tree to come crashing down between the cottage and the garage. Horror gave way to relief. "Gentlemen," Vladimír said, "I've never cut down a pine tree in my life, but I'm a machine fitter in the ČKD works in Vysočany, and that says it all!"

Another time, Vladimír and I set off to a place he'd always wanted to see, Doubrava, a village on either side of a single road that ends at the Labe River. After that, we cycled to Byšičky, where again, the only road into it goes around the circular village green and to leave the village, you have to go back the way you came, because, just as in Doubrava, the road ends there and in order to get ahead, you have to go back.

This is what we saw in Byšičky: villagers standing in their doorways, staring into a courtyard, boys sitting on the walls, staring into the same courtyard, heads peering over fences, staring into the courtyard from which came the scream of a circular saw. Vladimír could already sense that something had happened. We entered the yard, and I stopped and stared like the rest of them. In fact, I couldn't move. In the middle of the courtyard, a man was kneeling over a table saw, like a priest celebrating mass. The saw blade was still spinning, and the man's entire head, down to his neck, was buried in it, and since the blade had been set at a slight angle, the swath it had cut through the man's head was a centimeter wide. The table was awash in blood that glistened in the sunlight and the dead man's arms lay splayed in the slowly congealing pool. The onlookers seemed transfixed, because the sight was so tragic and so shockingly beautiful that it immobilized them, as though their limbs had been cast in plaster. It was Vladimír who ran to the saw, reached under the table and pressed the switch, and when he stood up, his hands were covered in blood, and as the voice of the saw died down, movement returned to the onlookers' limbs and they dispersed stiffly, as though they were all suffering from rheumatism. Only a handful came closer to the scene of the tragedy. Vladimír raised his arms into the shimmering light of day and shouted: "Don't touch anything till the police get here!" We rode away on our bicycles, Vladimír's shiny blood-soaked sleeves dried quickly in the sun. He held his head high as he cut through the air, and as always, he felt it an honor that fate had drawn him to a place of disaster.

When Bondy learned what had happened, he stared at the palms of his hands, his face turned red, but then he regained self-control: "I'm not going to let you upset me anymore. I have to climb to a place you can't follow, where I'll be invulnerable ... to the very pinnacle of Indian philosophy, where even Nirvana is a state of attachment. And since Vladimír is capable of anything, I'm going to kick away the ladder so you can't follow.

But the road to Doubrava that ends at the river, and to Byšičky that takes you around the village green so that the way forward and the way back are the same – that's something I want to see for myself. That is my road and that is my way. It's the way of Egon Bondy, goddamn it!"

*

Old Mrs. Šulcová, who emptied ash cans and dustbins and sold scrap paper and rags and metal to the recycling depot, grew very fond of Vladimír. She wore black gloves and put rouge on her cheeks and since she never washed it off, layers of the stuff built up and then flaked off, like puff pastry. She had the unshakable belief that Vladimír could be an Adventist minister and to get on his good side, she'd come round to clean house for him. Once she brought him an overcoat worn by a murdered man, a bricklayer who'd been stabbed in the back, and another time she brought him clothes that had belonged to a man who'd been killed and tossed into a pit of quicklime at a construction site. Yet another time she brought us a half bottle of rotgut liquor and after we'd drunk the stuff she told us she'd found it in a trash can. Once she brought us what looked like a modern sculpture meant to represent a cat or a dog, but then she whispered confidentially to Vladimír that there was a real cat inside it. Some pavers, just for fun, had thrown the cat into a vat of liquid concrete, then tossed it outside and the coating of cement hardened around the creature and it died inside its concrete shell.

Once, just after Christmas, Mrs. Šulcová told Vladimír that she had taken in some Gypsies and they got into a knife fight in the middle of the night and had stabbed her as well in the dark, so now she preferred to sleep in an abandoned shop, where she was happy enough, except that the place was infested with rats, and they were so hungry they ate the Christmas cake Vladimír had given her, even though she'd held it close to her body. And so one evening, when it was getting dark, Vladimír bought another Christmas cake and walked over to Kotlaska Street. At the corner of Na Žertvách we ran into Egon Bondy and when he saw the Christmas cake, he waved his hand dismissively. Vladimír told him all about Mrs. Šulcová, and how he'd cut up the coat with the fatal stab wound in it and pasted it onto a canvas so he could work the fabric into the painting. Then he left us, announcing that he intended to spend the night with Mrs. Šulcová so he could do battle with the rats over the Christmas cake. He said that next morning, he'd tell us how it turned out, because he wasn't about to let the rats get away with it.

*

One of the regulars in the World Cafeteria was a tailor who viewed the world through the prism of *The Protocols of the Elders of Zion*. One day he let Vladimír analyze his handwriting. Vladimír said that, judging by the way he formed his letters, the man was a loner who suffered from melancholia. "Your letter *b* tells me you should have been a forester, should have murdered your wife, buried her in the woods, and left her for others to find!" The tailor was so thrilled by the vision of his wife interred in the woods that he started calling Vladimír "an amazing straight shooter." At that moment a fight erupted among a bunch of Gypsies. It was pure histrionics, everything on the table swept to the floor. Mrs. Vlaštovková pulled the belligerents apart and kicked them out the door so forcefully they staggered across the square and collapsed in a heap under the monument to Julius Podlipny. No damage was done, except to a fist that had come in contact with the doorframe. A man sitting beside us was writing a letter. For half an hour, he kept wetting the tip of his pencil in his mouth, then he wrote the following sentence: "I offer you, honorably, both my hands." After the bar fight, Vladimír recalled what it felt like to be winded and have his knuckles bruised. "My brother and I had a fight like that," he said, "but we were brothers, so we butted heads and made up. That night, I had a cracked skull and an epileptic fit."

The letter writer wet his pencil again and wrote another sentence: "Dear Eugenia, let's try not to get on each other's nerves." He was an elderly man with a purple nose covered in purple veins as thick as worms. The tailor, still excited by Vladimír's reading of his handwriting, said: "You're an amazing straight shooter, and you have a nice jacket. The neck is a six, the back is a six, it's very fashionable in America. A centimeter below the navel, bring it down a bit, take three fingers off the waist." He brought out a tape measure, but when he tried to measure Vladimír's trousers and touched him in the crotch, Vladimír spilled his beer.

*

When Vladimír was going through his divorce, he met an army officer in the pub Za Větrem who bragged: "Do what I do. Take a belt to her!" A month later we met the same officer in the Bus Stop. He was hunched over and could barely see straight. "Join me in a glass," he said, and then tearfully, he explained: "My wife threw me out of the house, but before that, to show her how miserable I was, I dismantled her typewriter down to the very last screw, but she didn't get the point. I'll hang myself. I can't sleep and when I do, I sleep on my feet."

Then a man came in, opened up his shirt, and showed us a tracheal tube inserted in his larynx. He needed to confide in someone and Vladimír, always a wailing wall, asked him his name. The man pulled out a notebook and wrote: "Václav Kopecký." And then he wrote: "In two years I've had twenty-eight hundred injections, twenty-eight operations, on Monday they'll take the tube out and sew up the hole, my darling wife ran off with another man ... my nerves are shot ... she robbed me of five hundred crowns ... I know his name's Jarda ... but she's had others too and when I see her I'll have her arrested ..."

Mrs. Vlaštovková had a sunburn. Vladimír gave her a side-long glance, this giant of a woman who could slide glasses of draft Pilsner down the bar straight into the customer's hand. "What's with me?" she asked.

"You're a pink piglet, a peony about to shed its petals."

Mrs. Vlaštovková roared with laughter. "And what are you?"

"A weather station, with a scouring pad instead of a brain," Valdimír shot back.

A young man walked in and ran his eyes over the room, looking for someone to start a fight with, a prime example of the Czech brawler, a fellow always on the lookout for a hint of disrespect. No one on the horizon, so he kicked the door open and walked out, grim, hat pulled low over his eyes, searching for a victim. We went outside and walked past the railway crossing gates. A white climbing rose bush veiled the gate-keeper's booth.

Feeble-minded citizens were queuing up to buy the *Prague Evening News*. A jasmine blouse. A green skirt. Vladimír said to me: "Hey Doctor, look, I know you won't buy it for me, but I need paints, the colors they use for the Sunday edition of *Rudé Právo*. A dozen burnt siennas, two dozen blacks, a dozen vermillion reds, but I don't expect you'll buy them for me. Or will you? In that case, add in two dozen tubes of Paris blue, a dozen umbers, one white lead, but I don't expect you'll buy them for me. Or will you? In that case, another two dozen sheets of quarter imperial, and then you'll see! Back when I still trusted my girl," he said wistfully, "I longed to give her a bit of pleasure, so I strangled myself in front of her. But she took refuge with you again. Hah! She'd go swimming in the nude. At twelve noon! Anglers woud flub their casts, a cyclist ran off the embankment straight into the river. Well, you tell me what a body she had. Tell me! Swear to it! What? That afternoon she threw her sanitary pad into the toilet and I pulled it out with my bare hands. Of course I had every right to do it then because I was her husband, back then . . . I miss her, Doctor. What am I without her?"

And Vladimír walked back from Palmovka to the crossing gates, weeping, two rivulets of tears running down his cheeks, his head high, carrying his grief like a badge of honor, like a torch, and people walking past him, mostly women, turned to look at him, their nostrils flaring . . .

*

Whenever Vladimír felt pains in his chest, or rheumatism in his arms, he would buy a bottle of ordinary rye and rub it on his chest or his tennis elbow. When he had a sore throat, he would soak a kerchief in the rye and use it as a compress, and when he had a fever, we'd drink half the bottle, and pour the rest into a towel and wrap it around his chest, the way his grandmother used to do. With every advance and every pay packet, we already knew what kind of liquor we'd buy, and in fact we'd have it worked out almost a year in advance. We'd stand outside a liquor store window, considering our choices, arguing, trying to decide which of the liquor would best suit our current state of mind. Sometimes we'd buy two different kinds and mix them together. A bottle of cheap rum, for instance, is wonderful when you mix it with *griotka*, and it's particularly good when you mix it with green peppermint schnapps, a cocktail we called a "jockey." At other times, we'd mix rye with rum to make a so-called "bricklayer." Or we'd drink from each bottle separately, one glass at a time. It developed into a ritual. We'd lock the bottle in a sideboard the landlady had left behind, then we'd unlock it, ceremonially fill our glasses, then lock the bottle up again, nose the drink, clink glasses, and drink the liquor in a style appropriate to its quality. Sometimes we'd knock it back in one go, sometimes we'd sip it, praising its qualities, and when we'd drained the glasses, we'd write for a while and then, scarcely fifteen minutes later, we'd be standing in front of the sideboard and unlocking it, like a priest at the altar, and we'd be pouring each other another glass, amazed at how little of the liquor was left in the bottle. The bottle was like a holiday: at first, the time goes by slowly, but by the last week the days fly by as quickly as the glasses would vanish down our eager throats, because what we liked about these liquors was how we'd grow lighter and lighter, how our enthusiasm would mount, how we'd grin idiotically at each other and how the alcohol and the act of locking and unlocking the sideboard would bring us together until we'd both declare that we shouldn't really have poured that last glass ... Then we'd totter off, each to his own bed, observing closely how the alcohol would come to have an opposite effect in our guts and our heads, gradually transforming itself into sweet sleep, to be replaced next morning by a dull head.

We never shared a drop of the bottles we bought from our advances and pay packets with anyone else. We had other bottles for that. It was our secret, and if anyone came calling, we'd hide our glasses under our beds, and neither of us would swallow as much as a teardrop without the other, because it was our private business and ours alone, which is how, to this day, I drink my coffee. I have to drink it alone, like a sacrament, sipping it slowly, savoring it, smoking three strong cigarettes with it and thus inducing a lovely, meditative mood. If anyone shows up, I put out the cigarette, leave the coffee unfinished, and suspend the whole ritual, just as Vladimír and I would do when we opened and closed the beautiful sideboard. When Vladimír moved away from Libeň for good, I would open it in his honor and drink by myself, but without Vladimír, it was like ingesting an unconsecrated host. So I bought the sideboard from the landlady and with my hatchet, the one Vladimír used to hide from me, I chopped it up, bit by bit, and then burned it in the stove, listening to the pleasant sound of the flames roaring and consuming the wood steeped in liquor and memories ...

*

Like me, Vladimír knew how to talk to animals. Whenever he came across a cat, he'd hold out a finger and establish contact by touching its nose, and he'd say: "Doctor, if you become friends with animals you become friends with God, because you bring together the lowest with the highest in a single gesture and so close the circle. It's like when I whip up my graphics from all the debris on the factory floor, it's a short leap from there to the highest impulses of my soul. Ha ha!"

And so one day, we walked up past Kelerka, where there's a pond that was once surrounded by willows, and after stopping in at the Talking Dog pub – where there was an Alsatian that would tell customers to "Stuff it" and could clearly say the word "Crap" – we walked back through the Prosek cemetery. The entire expanse of consecrated ground was overgrown with ivy and we came to the Prosek chapel, which had recently turned almost a thousand years old. Since it was open, we went inside. A cleaning lady was dusting the pews and she had a beautiful tomcat with her, the kind I'm fond of, a tabby with white socks and a white bib and a pink nose. The cat was walking among the pews and when the cleaning lady knelt down to wipe the altar, the cat jumped up behind her on the pulpit and sat next to the altar bell that signals the Elevation of the Host. He looked like a ministrant or a sexton, or perhaps something superior. When the cleaning lady was done, she genuflected and the cat walked out behind her as she locked the chapel. Then she went into the rectory, the cat tagging along behind.

Later, Vladimír and I attended Sunday mass at the chapel and it was just as Vladimír had predicted. During high mass, the tomcat sat next to the altar bell and stared at the altar. We were sitting in the front pew and when we looked around, we could see that not a single face in the congregation showed a fraction of the piety and wisdom displayed by the cat, who was gazing fondly at the priest. Vladimír whispered that, through the priest, the cat was communing with God and God was communing with the cat, so that in special circumstances like this, cats were superior to lukewarm believers, and therefore heaven must be full of cats.

When Egon Bondy heard of Vladimír's observation, he said glumly: "Goddamn it! I'm going straight to bed. Where does that psychopath get this stuff? On second thought, I'm not going to bed, I'm going to collapse right here on the spot. Let an ambulance come and take me away, and not just any ambulance, I want the one with the flashing blue light on the roof. Sweet Jesus, it's going to be a long night!"

*

Once, in a pub called the Town of Rokycany, Vladimír suddenly grew still and stared into the corner. I looked at Vladimír and realized that something unusual was taking place there. "Rumen," Vladimír said. When I still didn't understand, he added, "Like swallows," and he wiggled his lower teeth with his index finger.

"Aha," I said, without turning around. "A mother is spooning porridge from a dish and warming it up in her mouth before she . . ."

"Or cooling it down," said Vladimír.

"And then she's feeding her baby mouth-to-mouth," I went on.

Vladimír nodded and said, "No."

I shook my head and insisted: "Yes. Aha," I said. "Two lovers are French kissing and she's pleading with him to transfer his saliva to her."

Vladimír shook his head and said, "Yes."

I nodded in delight and said, "No."

"Doctor," Vladimír said, "promise me that when I reach that

stage of life, you'll do the same for me."

"I promise," I said, shaking my head. Then I turned around to see what it was that had attracted Vladimír's attention. Two friends were sitting at a table, one was chewing vigorously, and the other was just moving his mouth back and forth. Then I saw what they were doing. The man who'd been chewing vigorously would spit a mouthful of mushy salami onto a plate, and the other, clearly toothless, would use a knife and fork to eat what his friend had chewed up for him.

"That wall in Ungelt," I said.

Vladimír thought for a moment, then shook his head, but because he was smiling, I knew he was seeing what I saw, the fresco in Ungelt of an old man suckling at the breast of a beautiful young woman.

"A crisis situation," Vladimír said.

"And during the war?" I asked.

"It was horrible," Vladimír muttered in a half whisper. "You know, I'd like to try it some day."

*

Using a telescope, Vladimír was observing the ravens wheeling slowly over Libeň, past the Chateau, and toward Chabry. He put the instrument down and said: "Doctor, ravens and crows are the smartest birds in the world. None of your flying in flocks, none of your quasi-military formations in the sky. They just drift about any way they feel like, and they always manage to get where they're going. And look how modest they are. They're like black Diogeneses. When they land on a field, they feed on the crops, and if the crops have been brought in, they comb through the stubble and when that's picked clean they get into the baled straw or the manure pile and it's good enough for them. And now I'm going to put on my rabbi's hat and wear it like a raven on my head. They nest and hatch by the thousands in the trees around Baron Chotek's chateau in Veltrusy and come winter, the trees around the Bohnice asylum are full of them and the crazies call them 'Bohnice chickens.' Old ravens have a nose for gunpowder and as soon as anyone gets near them with a rifle, off they fly. And then, Doctor – Doctor – have you ever seen a raven run over on the road? I haven't. Swallows, thrushes, pheasants, quail, rabbits, yes, but never a raven. And why do you suppose that is? Their radar is so precise that they slowly lift off just before they're about to be mown down. If I had a brain like a raven, I'd be pissing out graphics fifty years ahead of their time. As I say, Doctor, the raven, that's my bird."

We went for a walk and stopped for beer at the Ship, a pub run by Mr. Müller, the father of the fastest hockey player in the country, the one they brought back dead from Garmisch-Partenkirchen, and no one knew how it happened. Vladimír observed Mr. Müller closely for a long time, but he seemed in good spirits and poured beer and made jokes as though nothing had happened. "That's the way it should be," said Vladimír, with satisfaction. "Like the ravens," he added, but when the ventilator sucked the smoke out of the air, a photograph of a curly-haired hockey player came into view on the wall. He was leaning forward on his stick and his skates shone as brightly as his hair and his smile was as broad as his blades were long. A small band of black ribbon lay across the corner of the frame.

Mr. Müller rinsed out the glasses and, glancing at the photograph, said: "Every time I look at it my eyes well up."

*

In Libeň, at No. 24, the Embankment of Eternity, the back of the little courtyard where Vladimír and I lived had once housed a blacksmith's workshop. It had been built as an afterthought and no direct sunlight could reach it, so paradoxically, at dusk or when it was overcast, our two rooms were bright enough that we didn't have to turn on the lights, but when the sun beat down onto the facades and rooftops of the buildings across the street, the glare made our rooms so gloomy we had to switch the lamps on. To add to the paradox, our flat was chilliest in May and June, when the walls were still radiating cold from the winter months, and anyone who went from the warm courtyard into our flat would shudder, as though he'd just walked into a refrigerator. But in winter, the marlstone walls radiated the warmth they'd absorbed during the hot summer months and we didn't have to heat the rooms. Vladimír didn't heat his room in the winter anyway, only in summer, during cold spells.

At the time Vladimír was studying Leonardo da Vinci and because he too wanted to become an inventor and an innovator, he installed what he called Vladimír's system of window mirrors, which proved very successful. Somewhere I found, or appropriated – how I can't remember – ten large oblong mirrors that fit exactly between the inner and outer windows of our flat and on the sill so that the light from the courtyard reflected onto the ceiling and lit the rooms so brightly that visitors were startled. Vladimír took the mirrors that were left over, and using small nails, he attached them on the inside of the glass panels in two doors, two panels per door. Anyone who came in and then wanted to leave became disoriented, because they saw part of the room behind them in the mirror in front of them. Not only that, Vladimír attached to the back wall two enormous mirrors, salvaged from restaurants that had been closed down. They extended across the length of the room so that anyone looking in from the courtyard would be confused to see two of Vladimír or me, or a large crowd, if there were three of us in the room.

And thus it happened that when Mrs. Šulcová came to clean for us, free of charge – it was she who thought Vladimír should enter the priesthood and brought him clothes that had once belonged to murder victims – and she walked in and set her bucket and rags down next to the door and, with her hand still on the door handle, she carried on about divine calling she'd dreamt about that night, and about Vladimír, the mirror on the door so confused her that she thought the bucket reflected in the mirror was actually in the corridor, and she leaned forward to pick it up and her forehead hit the mirror with a tremendous whack. When she realized the bucket was there at her feet, she picked it up. Then she saw herself in the huge mirror on the back wall, holding the bucket, and she walked straight toward it and Vladimír had to guide her back to the doorway so she could start washing the door, but when she looked in the mirror on the door and saw the reflection of her bucket, she bent over again to pick it up and her hand scrabbled against the glass the way kittens do when they want out, and in the end, still thinking the bucket standing at her feet was in the mirror, she tripped over it and bumped her head so hard against the door that we decided to empty the bucket and take her outside, not just into the courtyard, but out of the building altogether, and even there her movements were so erratic that Vladimír walked her back to the shop where, the previous Christmas, the rats had come out at night and eaten her Christmas cake.

When Egon Bondy saw Vladimír's system with the mirrors and heard our stories about Mrs. Šulcová, he cried: "Aha! You're expecting me to rise to the bait! I, who have translated Morgenstern?" And because he was always afraid that all the taverns would close in the evening, he brought in jugs and buckets of beer while it was still daylight, just in case. Then he sat in a chair and lectured us about Surrealism and Dostoyevsky, one leg crossed over his knee, all the while regarding himself in the mirrors. He couldn't seem to get enough of himself, and he even seemed transfixed by his own reflection in the large mirror on the back wall, admiring himself, lowering his eyes and then raising them again, the better to savor his own image.

Around midnight, when we were all in bed, I was awakened by a noise that sounded like water running out of a tap. I turned on the light and there was Egon, having drunk fifteen beers, contentedly pissing away the remains of the thirteenth on the carpet. "Can't you do that outside, you idiot?" I said. He lay down again and replied: "What, and run into a mirror?" And he went contentedly back to sleep, while his little shoes glistened in the enormous pool of urine like two boats floating on an ocean inlet. Enraged, I got up and urinated into both his shoes.

Next morning, when Egon woke up, we were long since at

work. He stood by the door, absorbed in his thoughts, look-ing into the mirror and stroking his beard and all at once, as he stared absently into the mirror, he caught sight of his two shoes. "Goddamn it, who put them out in the corridor? It must have been Vladimír!" he shouted, and as he bent over to pick them up, he bashed his forehead against the mirror. First, he looked around to see if Mr. Kaifr, who had just come off the night shift, was still asleep, then he quietly put on his shoes and, just as quietly, walked out the door.

That afternoon I bought three kilos of cabbage to scrub the damp pool of the poet's piss from the landlady's imitation Persian rug. And I smiled, because I was fond of Egon Bondy, perhaps even fonder than I was of Vladimír, and that's saying something.

*

Once, Vladimír and I set out for Hradové Střímelice where we were told the oldest female pubkeeper in Central Europe resided. She'd been at the pub ninety-one years, drawing beer, reciting Vítězslav Hálek, and she knew whole passages from gothic novels by heart. Vladimír was thrilled. She saved her best stories for Vladimír. For twenty years, she told him, she'd been so busy she couldn't go to confession, so she wrote down all her sins and when the priest came to give her absolution, he had to perform the ceremony on a ladder, because she was standing on it, washing the windows.

We drank some green liquor and then a parade of people in masks and costumes filed by, and viewed from inside the murky taproom, they looked like Tyrolean tablecloths stained with colorful jams and jellies. Every so often the face of the old woman would emerge from the dim light. Her clothes were as dark as the gloom, so we could see only her face and the glasses of beer she was carrying.

Later, when we walked down the hill to Čerčany to catch the train, we passed a woman standing by a farm gate, but we could only see her when she moved. The gate behind her was green, with horizontal gray slats, and the woman was wearing a green striped dress, so what stood out against the gate was her face, a white death mask. We jumped over a creek coming out of the woods, a tiny stream flowing over a shallow sandy riverbed, and we could see a bonfire in the distance and the people in masks were singing and dancing in the flickering light, shouting like pagans. Vladimír was transfixed. The man who had led the parade carrying the club flag was now lying on his back in the shallow creek drunk and smiling, the flag covering his chest, oblivious to the world. A blanket of water a few centimeters deep rippled over him as he lay there, his head resting on a smooth round slab of flint, breathing contentedly in and out while the water undulated the flag.

*

One time, when Vladimír and I were obsessed with obscenity and looking for material we could use to write an homage to Georg Grosz, we collected graffiti from the washrooms in factories and pubs, and we'd already recorded several dozen of them when we blundered by mistake into the ladies' room at the train station in Veleslavín. Some attendants burst in on us and to avoid a confrontation we locked ourselves in a stall. They raised the alarm and the mayor of the town showed up. We unlocked the door and everyone came at us as though we were perverts, accusing us of hanging around in the washroom, lying in wait for young schoolgirls so we could molest them. When we showed them the graffiti we'd already gathered from every possible kind of public toilet, the mayor took back his initial accusation but then insisted that we were homosexuals intent on satisfying our lust in the Veleslavín washrooms, and that collecting pornographic graffiti was just a pretext to throw them off the scent. Then he spit in our faces, and so did the attendants, because ordinary people hold homosexuality in extraordinary contempt.

This experience merely strengthened our resolve to go on collecting graffiti. One day, we got into the women's washroom at the Faculty of Arts, to which we'd gained access by feigning interest in a lecture series on African revolutions. The inscriptions we found there drove Vladimír wild. He said: "I thought I was the only one with such lascivious thoughts. Now I see it's commonplace."

When Egon Bondy heard about all this, he wrung his hands, raised both arms over his head, and wailed: "Jesus, you two miscreants are stealing my thunder and you don't even know you're doing it. Just now I've been sweating out a sentence: Sexus is anonymous; Eros has an addressee. We're all in the same sexual boat, but everyone sails under his own erotic flag. Goddamn it! I'll have to swallow a kilo of pills again tonight, just to get a little sleep!"

*

Vladimír was perpetually guileless. Once he came to visit us in Nymburk with his wife, Tekla, who then accompanied my father in his truck to pick up a Škoda 420 that had broken down.

We awaited their return on the banks of the Labe, and when the truck pulled up, Vladimír was so moved he wept. My father was driving the truck, with Tekla behind the wheel of the Škoda 420, copying my father's exact moves with the steering wheel as he did a three-point turn and backed into the yard. Then she and Vladimír went swimming down by the towpath. Mother and the schoolmaster's wife watched them though a telescope and saw Vladimír, at ten thirty on a Sunday morning, just when high mass was about to begin, making love to Tekla under transparent sheets of river water. The schoolmaster, Cyril, also took a look through the telescope and said wistfully: "I rather suspect this generation won't be following in the footsteps of Comenius."

Later, when I took Vladimír gently to task for what he had done in the river while high mass was going on, he laughed out loud and said: "I knew I was being watched, but I wanted to give your mother pleasure."

When he heard about it, Egon Bondy put his hands over his ears and shouted: "Damn it, Doctor, enough's enough! Vladimír is fulfilling the biblical prophecy. Many shall come from the east and west, and shall sit down with Abraham, and Isaac, and Jacob. Vladimír's a pure, absolute lunatic."

*

Once we were sitting in the pub U Brabců and talking about the expanding universe while drinking beer in a manner appropriate to the topic of conversation. Oh, that Vladimír! He never went to the pissoir on his own initiative, and if he were visiting someone, he would never go to the toilet, even if his bladder were about to burst. And so after we'd had five beers and made our first trip to the toilets, we came back to find two brothers sitting at our table, talking animatedly. The one wearing dark glasses was doing most of the talking. He had a booming voice and every syllable was so beautifully articulated we just listened to the melody of his speech. Vladimír was nibbling delicately at a bun, because all his teeth had come loose. But when our two table companions got up together to go to the pissoir, we saw that the one with the booming voice was blind. When they returned, our conversations merged and we learned that when the two brothers were children, they were horsing around, jumping from trees, and one of them let go of a branch and it snapped back into the other's eyes, blinding him.

Afterward, when we were standing at the streetcar stop and Vladimír had pried sixty hellers out of me for the fare, he said: "One day, when I'm up to it, I'll ask the blind fellow if, the moment he was blinded, his eyes turned inward and gave him his one and only look at his own eye sockets."

Next day, we sat in the Slovanská Lipa pub in Vysočany and Vladimír complained that he was going blind, that his trigeminal nerve was pressing against his temple, and he feared that a hard sneeze would knock his front teeth out. He grabbed his head, felt it all over, and then predicted that a storm was coming. As usual, a five-inch nail had been driven into his head and he could feel the point with his tongue. Moreover, the day before yesterday, he'd been competing with the apprentices over who could leap from a standing start onto a workbench with a slab of iron laying on top of it. Vladimír won the contest but gashed his shin on the overhanging slab and now he went back and forth between massaging his shin, grabbing his side, pressing a finger against his trigeminal nerve, and wiggling his front teeth to see just how loose they'd become.

At this point, a man at the next table got up and started talking, while casting side glances at the clock on the wall. "My name is Duže," he said, "like 'duše,' soul. Just repeat as often as you can: 'Be calm, be calm, be calm.' If you have any need for hypnotherapy, I live in Horní Počernice, anyone can tell you how to find me. I live just past the garden." The big hand on the clock now showed one minute to nine, and Mr. Duže said: "Excuse me, but I'm going to miss my bus," and he left in a hurry but in the swinging doors he collided with the waiter who was just spinning round with a tray of foaming beer. Mr. Duže fell, drenched and blinded, and ended up on all fours in a pool of beer, screaming and cursing. Vladimír rose to the occasion. He stood up, buttoned his overcoat, leaned over Mr. Duže and said quietly: "Just repeat after me: Be calm, be calm, be calm. If you need anything, my name is Vladimír and I work in ČKD. Anyone can tell you how to find me. I'm in the building at the far end."

Another time we were sitting in the taproom U Horkých in the Jewish quarter of Libeň and we each ordered ten bread rolls and chased each one with a glass of Smíchov beer. The pub was buzzing with conversation and laughter and some spruced-up women workers were sitting over by the window, drinking coffee with shots of rum, when a man came over to our table and said: "Gentlemen, I'm a married man, which in and of itself isn't that interesting, but my wife and I are living with my father-in-law in a single room that's divided down the middle by a curtain, and I can tell you, gentlemen, the fact that my father-in-law eats my food isn't that interesting in and of itself, but at night, when I have sex with my wife on one side of the curtain, I can see my father-in-law's silhouette on the curtain right next to our heads and he's jerking off so skillfully that when I start to come, so does he. I ask you, gentlemen, where else in the world could you find a father-in-law like that? My name isn't important. I'm just a housepainter."

When Egon Bondy heard about the man blinded by a branch, he dismissed it as insignificant, and when he heard about Mr. Duže and Vladimír, he rubbed his hands as if he were delighted that our once phenomenal encounters were beginning to lose their intensity. Then, when he heard about the father-in-law who masturbated beside his own daughter as she was making love, he took me by the shoulder and looked at me skeptically, then took my head in his hands and peered intently into my eyes to see if I was telling the truth. Then he shouted: "Where is he?"

"Vladimír's probably home by now," I said.

"I mean the painter!" Bondy shouted. "Where is he?" And he shook his fist in my face. "Don't play games with me. I know what you're up to. You're trying to put me off writing, but you are way off beam, goddamn it! You've simply got to introduce me to that painter!"

"Right now he's painting that big radio and TV transmission tower," I said. "He's hanging by a rope with a paintbrush in his hand, dipping it into the paint and singing."

"Bring him here!" Bondy yelled, plugged his ears, and wailed: "Vladimír has to write all this down, and if he doesn't, then you have to do it, just as Božena Němcová did with her fairy tales and Jirásek with his old Czech legends. And tell Vladimír for me: the closer a mountain is to the sun, the colder it gets at the top. And only the sun has the right to its spots, as Goethe once said of Frederick, the Prussian king, whom I happen to be studying at the moment. But you've got to introduce me to that painter! Don't you see? He could be a martyr in disguise. That's the whole point. The Pope can say, 'The church has no need of martyrs!' But we need them more than ever, so bring me that painter, goddamn it!"

*

Once I went to visit Vladimír, who at the time was living on Kostnické Square, on the fourth floor. When Vladimír's mother opened the door for me, I could see the tears in her eyes, glistening in the dim light of the foyer. Then a door flew open and a casserole dish came sailing out of the room and tipped on its side. The sheer force of the throw propelled the contents out of it, shiny boiled cabbage followed by four or five dumplings, as round as beer mats. It all flew out the open door and down the lighted corridor, and the ballistics of it carried it right to Mrs. Boudníková's door.

"How wonderful of you to come for a visit!" she shouted down the hall. "Vladimírek will be thrilled," then adding quietly: "We've had quite a night. It was dreadful how he carried on." And then, out loud: "But you look splendid, Doctor, you must have been for a swim" ... and then quietly: "It was quite a to-do, and you could hear it all through the building ..." and then more loudly: "Come right in! Vladimír has a new sweater. He'll be thrilled you came." And quietly: "He smashed into the mirror and cut himself, then smeared blood over the wall and on a big pad of paper, where he wrote: 'I shall become the priest of madness ...'"

I found Vladimír in a depressed state. All he would say was: "Mother was complaining that since she's feeding me, I should be a little more grateful, and so I threw the casserole out the door."

I said: "That was magnificent, just like when Salvador Dalí had himself photographed in midair while someone dumped a whole aquarium of water, including the fish, on him, and cats were flying through the air with tobacco pouches tied to their tails to drive them crazy."

Vladimír was ecstatic. "So you saw that casserole dish in the air, and the cabbage, and the light. Wasn't it beautiful?"

I said it certainly was, and that we were going for a beer to the Rose Bush where the pubkeeper and his wife each have their own budgies and the budgies get into terrible squabbles and the pubkeeper and his wife merely look on and smile, because instead of arguing with each other, the budgies do it for them.

When I told Egon Bondy about the casserole incident, he was nonplussed, but then he grew excited: "Goddamn it! Nietzsche wondered where the barbarians of the twentieth century were. Well, it's Vladimír! Vladimír, a barbarian of the twentieth century, swimming in the cold water of art and the warm water of science, as Dalí put it. Vladimír . . ."

*

Once, as Vladimír and I were walking through the countryside along the Labe River, we saw a tall, solitary tree exposed to the sun. Behind it was a dark forest. Vladimír stood looking at it intently, then smiled and nodded as if he were agreeing with himself. "Look," he said. "That tree is Goethe. He had the right conditions, his hair was shaggy, he soaked up the Hellenic sun from every direction, and his roots drew what they needed from the earth. Me, I'm a tree in those woods back there. My shoulders are worn down, my skimpy crown has to make do with only as much sunshine as can make it through to me, we rub up against each other and get in each other's way, yet we are alive. But," Vladimír went on, "I say that thanks to the imagination and to tactile experience, I'm just as shaggy as Goethe here," pointing to the lone tree. "I have eliminated the difference between strong individuality and the masses." And he burst out laughing. That's when I understood that Vladimír's lithographs were the apotheosis of the fourth estate, the working class, that because our branches are constantly in touch with one another, we are condemned to live in thrall to the Universe and Beauty.

As Vladimír stood there before that lone tree, deeply moved, he went on speaking, tenderly: "Everything in my graphic art is grounded, like this tree here. To me, this tree is made of glass and I can see the sap rise by osmosis, I can see the liquid flowing through the capillaries to the branches, I can see the blossoms and the fruit. Even the ground is transparent to me and made of glass. I can follow precisely where the roots and fibers go, I can see how they draw sustenance from soil and water, I can see the entire glass tree, and I can also see each of its phases at any season of the year, and here and now. I can see every circle around which every part of the tree rotates. What I'm seeing is the harmony of forces and fluids. A little imagination and everything becomes clearer and therefore more human, do you see what I mean, Doctor? Do you understand?"

And at that moment I realized how beautifully structured Vladimír's graphic art is, how grounded it is, like any decent radio, any telephone, like the tanks on gasoline trucks that drag a piece of sparking chain on the pavement behind them so the fuel inside won't explode. And I saw how Vladimír too, when he's broken, can always pick himself up again, when he bends down and touches the earth with his finger it renews his powers, powers that he draws on in a mystical, yet utterly real way.

When Egon Bondy heard what Vladimír had said on our walk, he kicked a radiator in the World Cafeteria and split open his tiny shoe and then, holding his foot in his hand, he hopped around on one leg and shouted: "About that tree, it's old Jakub Böhme, that brilliant little squirt from Zhořelec who dug away the earth from the roots of a tree so he could understand how matter is related to thought, and it allowed him to declare: 'Der menschgewordene Gott' – God, who has become Man. But that's Vladimír for you! Why, that tree is the substratum of Hegel's entire philosophy. I've had to study it for a whole year and Vladimír, the bastard, just blurts it out when he's out for a stroll, as easily as blowing his nose. I'm telling you, it's pure insanity. And I've ruined my shoe. You'll buy me a new pair! But enough of that!" said Bondy.

Egon Bondy then decided to devote himself completely and utterly to art. To avoid the legal obligation to be gainfully employed, he decided to have himself committed. After the first day in the asylum, he was enthralled. "Hey, Vladimír, Vladimír, you'd love it here. A nice little institution, close to Prague, cosy and warm inside, good, hearty food, and they'd even give you a box of paints and paper or canvas and let you out from time to time, and you can create. And if you feel like going crazy, well, you'd be certified and the authorities couldn't touch you!"

But there was no way Vladimír would leave his job at the factory, because the factory meant more to him than a mental institution. It was an asylum, a sanctuary, a school, a mistress. So he rejected the idea. A month later Egon Bondy showed up, and if he'd been pale before, now he was tanned, wind-burned, but also out of sorts. He flopped down on the couch and shouted: "Goddamn it! Screw the nuthouse! They've introduced Soviet methods. They now believe the best cure for minor mental disorders is work therapy. I have my own hoe and every day I have to go out and hoe sugar beets. I'm getting healthier by the day, but good health is a veritable death sentence to poetry!" Then he fell asleep. He slept for three hours and when he woke up, he asked me: "Doctor, might there be a little milk around? And some rye bread to go with it?"

*

Vladimír decided he was going to take up high diving. In preparation, he made his own bathing suits, which he spent days sewing, one from bandages and the other from shiny black cotton. They were basically two triangles joined together by thin cotton tapes, but the coverage had to be precise. Vladimír sewed away, then tried the suits on and checked them out in the big mirror. He even bought himself an inexpensive hand mirror so he could see how the suits fit from behind.

When Vladimír dove from the high board in Poldolí, it was a real occasion. He had never dived before, just as he never played the violin or the mandolin and yet when he took them up he would play them with great feeling. It was wonderful watching Vladimír enthusiastically set off at a run along the board, land hard on the end of it with both feet, rise into the air and spread his arms, then gradually pull them close to his body, bend at the waist and finally, his six-foot-six body would plunge into the water. Moments later his head would reappear above the surface and after a couple of strokes, he'd slap his hands on the edge of the pool, water trickling down his face, and dispense advice to the boys watching him: "Look, the main thing when you dive is to keep your eye on the spires of Vyšehrad. At first, it looks as if they're sinking, but then you reach the top of your arc, as you do your tuck and go head-down, keep looking out of the corner of your eye and you'll see that, as you're plunging toward the water, Vyšehrad will suddenly, at the same speed, shoot up toward the horizon. Why am I telling you this? You must always be mindful of what you are doing, and at the same time, of what's going on around you."

Then Vladimír got out of the water and again, seriously and almost as if conducting a scientific experiment, he would mount the steps to the highest board, run forward, and compel Vyšehrad in the background to descend slightly and then suddenly shoot upward as his eyes and his body experienced those legendary dives from the highest board.

When Bondy learned of this, he was fuming. "Goddamn it! Vladimír is constantly trying to show me up. To match that, I'd have to jump headfirst into an empty swimming pool, or dive from the spire of St. Vitus's Cathedral. When I tell Zbyněk Fišer about this, he'll be flabbergasted."

*

I once lent Vladimír a pamphlet outlining why the Hungarian national soccer team was the best in the world, and why it had won the match of the century against England. Vladimír returned the pamphlet to me in a jubilant mood: "Doctor, you've made me very happy. The so-called Hidegkuti maneuver, his ability to turn on a dime and change the course of the entire game, that's exactly what my active graphics do in the same space."

When I told this to Egon Bondy, he was silent for a while and seemed to shrink by a few inches. Then he said in a low, tired voice: "I've said it before, but Vladimír is completely insane. Comparing his active graphics to Hidegkuti's footwork? Well, I won't breathe a word of it to Zbyněk Fišer. He'd scold me for not coming up with it myself ..."

*

Once Vladimír fell in love with a plump girl from Čimice. During a break at the Poldi steelworks, to demonstrate his regard for her, he set up the drop hammer to stop at a precise point just above his nose. Then he lay down on his back, stuck his head into the device and had a friend press the release. The heavy drop hammer came crashing down and stopped abruptly touching the tip of Vladimír's nose. That was how Vladimír prepared for his afternoon rendezvous with the girl he was in love with. Later, at twilight, as he walked with her along the Čimice road, he undid his tie, attached it to the bough of an apple tree, then quickly wound it around his neck and partially hung himself, while the girl fled home through the gathering dark. Next day, Vladimír came back to the same grove of trees near Čimice, where his tie was still hanging from the branch, and he reenacted his declaration of love while a photographer took a picture of him with his tongue hanging out.

I was sitting at home in my bathrobe and slippers when Vladimír told me the story and showed me the photos. I shook my head and tried to drive away the sound of the drop hammer crashing to a sudden halt and the vision of him hanging by his tie. Vladimír said: "What was I supposed to do to make the girl happy? I was giving her something she'd never forget."

When I told this to Egon Bondy, he plugged his ears and stamped his feet and shouted: "Enough, Doctor, that's enough, for God's sake. These stories about Vladimír sap my strength and I go flat like a punctured tire, so for mercy's sake, Doctor, enough is enough! I'm gimping along on bare rims already! The bastard has punched a hole in my soul! Goddamn it!"

*

Vladimír would bring over a friend from work by the name of Kadel. He was always teasing Kadel, not for his own enjoyment, but because he thought it would do him good. They'd arrive and Kadel would be quite alarmed. "Kadel, did you notice that we were followed by a guy in a chauffer's hat?" Vladimír said.

Kadel nodded and looked around nervously. He wore, as he always did, a hat with big ear lugs so he wouldn't catch a cold. "If anything should happen, Kadel, where was it you said you wanted to be buried? Was it Zbraslav, or Modřany?" Vladimír would put his finger to his lips, then tiptoe to the door, fling it open, and dash out into the courtyard. When he came back, Kadel's eyes would be full of questions, the two men would shake hands, look each other in the eye, and swear that if anything should happen, they had heard nothing and seen nothing.

The journey back from work would always be full of mystery

and intrigue, and when they'd arrive, Kadel would be almost prostrate with terror. His hair would be standing on end, his brow damp, but when he looked at Vladimír, I could see he couldn't live without him. Or perhaps he could, but he and Vladimír had secrets, not just by day, but by night too. They were surrounded by danger.

Once, they were holding hands in my room at No. 24, the Embankment of Eternity, when Vladimír suddenly ran into the courtyard to see if anyone was there, then he declared solemnly: "Kadel, from now on our password will be: From the Punkva to the Dnieper!" And then Vladimír sat down and casually said: "Look, Kadel, I think you should put on warm underwear and an undershirt now. It's cold in prison, did you know that?" Or: "Kadel, do you have a pain at the back of your neck? I don't want to alarm you, but did you know that a sore neck is how paralysis begins?" And: "Look, Kadel, have you made your final arrangements?" And: "What do you think Kadel, would you rather be eaten alive by a shark or by quicklime?" And then they would walk out together into the night.

One time, Vladimír came home by himself in a state of great excitement. "Doctor, who would have thought it of Kadel? I've run out of intrigues and secret passwords to keep him occupied, so I tried to teach him how to make Explosionalist graphics and he got so upset he took a set of heavy iron calipers that weigh more than a kilo, straightened them out, and threw them at me, they grazed the hair by my ears and stuck in the wardrobe door and wobbled there for a while. Who'd have thought it? That boy has a personality almost like mine. He thrilled me, throwing those calipers at me."

When Egon Bondy heard this, he looked at me askance and

said calmly: "I'm not going to let this upset me anymore. From the Punkva to the Dnieper? Vladimír rules the earth ... or something. Thank goodness I've already written *Prager Leben*, or my *Small Book* and my *Large Book* and some other little books of poetry. But what am I supposed to do? We're gradually downing our writing tools, locking our typewriter in the cupboard. Zbyněk Fišer and I are going to take up Indian philosophy. Zbyněk Fišer will teach me Sanskrit, the train will enter the tunnel, and after a couple of years sowing the seeds of mysticism, I'll begin to sprout green again ... So, from the Punkva to the Dnieper? For mercy's sake, Doctor, why does Vladimír torment me? But so be it. Goddamn it!"

*

When the director of the Crooked Wheel gallery saw Vladimír's graphics at the poet Jiří Kolář's place, he decided on the spot to organize a show in Warsaw. Vladimír folded the works, for which they had no export permit, unbuttoned his trousers and shirt, laid the sheets against his stomach, did up his trousers and shirt again, and flew from Prague to the Crooked Wheel gallery in Warsaw. And since there was no paper available in Warsaw to print a catalog, Jiří Kolář discovered that you could airmail a parcel weighing up to four and a half kilograms to Warsaw, so they cut and wrapped several parcels of wrapping paper weighing four and a half kilograms each and mailed them from different post offices around the outskirts of Prague to the Crooked Wheel, Warsaw, to the attention of Mr. Bogusz, who then used the paper to print the catalogs. And at that same exhibition, a Mr. Bernard Davis, director of a modern art museum in Miami, saw Vladimír's lithographs, and before long those lithographs were flying across the Atlantic, where they were given a celebrated showing.

From that time on, Vladimír lived in fear of having his hair cut. Whenever he saw scissors in the hands of a barber he froze. What if the barber worked on lithographs of his own every evening and was jealous of Vladimír and suddenly decided to plunge his scissors into Vladimír's eyes and into his brain? That was why Vladimír had his mother and later, his beloved wife, Tekla, cut his hair.

Every haircut was an event in itself. Voices were raised and many mirrors deployed before Vladimír was satisfied that his hair was cut so that it appeared not to have been cut. He loved a dandyish haircut and the casual negligence in dress of a Baudelaire or a Beau Brummell. But when they were short of cash, and Tekla would cut up his clothes, tearing them into strips she could sell for scrap, she'd frequently threaten to go after Vladimír's eyes with the scissors. And so every time Tekla would cut Vladimír's hair, he imagined that when she was done, he'd be blind, because as she cut, Tekla would brandish the scissors like a fencing foil, while scolding Vladimír for not bringing more money home and asking him why they only had a total of two crowns fifty in ready cash.

When Egon Bondy learned of this, his chin sank and his legendary, bright-red lower lip glistened like the inside of a cherry, his blue eyes shifted sorrowfully to one side as he declared: "Everyone knows that air moves freely across borders, that water flows, that the birds of the air can fly where they will without passports, but for mercy's sake, what am I supposed to make of Vladimír's work stashed away in someone's trousers, flying across state borders, without permission, like a god? That's almost acceptable, but why do I have to know about those amazing incidents with the scissors? No woman has ever wanted to prick out my eyes for love. What have I been doing wrong?"

*

Vladimír liked pubs that were heated with coal or wood in a Musgraves 14 stove, or one of those enormous black Fil'akovo stoves that looked like a fireproof safe. Once we were sitting by the window in the pub U Horkých, snow was falling outside, and Vladimír was casting a melancholy glance into the taproom where the bartender, Mr. Šoler, was stoking the stove, whistling away, and drawing his legendary glasses of Smíchov beer. It had been snowing since morning, and two groups of boys appeared outside, throwing snowballs at each other. One group, outpelted by the other, began to retreat.

Vladimír said: "That stove over there in the corner is me, and if you don't stoke me, I won't give off heat. But now, watch this," he said, glancing out the window at the boys pelting each other with snowballs. He ran outside into the snow, just as he was, and first he bent over, then put his elbows in the snow and went down on all fours, making a bench of his back. "This is it," I said to myself. "He's finally gone mad, just as Egon Bondy predicted. Pure insanity, a classic schizo."

Vladimír, however, smiled, turned toward the window, where the customers were looking out, some with pity, others indignantly. But Vladimír went on smiling that bright smile he would always give when he was faced with a mystery about to be revealed. And I began to laugh as well, because as the boys in the snowball fight were retreating, one of them backed up dangerously close to Vladimír, who was waiting there patiently, the way astronomers wait for a solar eclipse they'd predicted down to the second. And that's exactly what happened. Without ever having to shift his position on all fours in the snow, Vladimír was there for the eclipse. One of the retreating boys, in the act of throwing a snowball, tumbled backward over Vladimír like a soccer player executing a scissors kick, and fell on his back and, shocked by the unexpected obstacle, remained lying there. Vladimír pulled him to his feet, then picked up a handful of snow, gently packed it into a ball and the boy joined in, the tide turned and soon the boys in the other group couldn't fend off the one-man advantage and took to their heels around the building where the confectioner, Václav Šimůnka, once had a corner store that sold tallow, his sign still visible on the gable of the building.

*

Once Vladimír spent a week on a voluntary labor brigade. He came back full of enthusiasm and sanctimony, but he was limping. "Doctor, it was magnificent," he told me. "I spent the whole day with my hands in the earth, harvesting potatoes, and I had the whole world within me, mother earth, soil. But then, oh, what a delight. I'm bent over, tying my shoelaces, and suddenly, I feel a huge bump and I'm flying ten meters through the air. When I land, I turn around, and I'm staring at an angry ram. You know how it is, almost all males are jealous of me. The herder, a German, runs up and says: "He does that," and then he drives his flock of sheep on past us. It was magnificent. I only fainted once. One evening, I'm sitting there on a bench, washing my feet in a wooden tub and all at once a farmhand drives a herd of cattle past. One of the cows looks over at me and starts running straight at me, just the way women come on to me. I look up, and by this time the cow has plowed to a stop and is breathing on me and drooling on my knee, then she dips her head down, drinks all the water in the tub, and licks my toes. The herdsman comes up and tries to explain: "There's not much water around. It's just what she does." And I fainted. I've never had my toes licked before. I'm telling you, Doctor, next chance I get, I'm going to volunteer again."

Later, when Vladimír got married a second time and went with his bride on a honeymoon, he took her on a voluntary labor brigade to harvest potatoes. He came back disappointed. "Doctor, I'm telling you, fortune has turned her back on me. No ram, no thirsty cow, just bad luck. Nothing happened. As I say, fortune has abandoned me, maybe for good."

When Egon learned about the jealous ram and the thirsty cow, he gently butted his head against the wall, right there in the street, and pounded the plaster with both fists and shouted: "Goddamn it! Vladimír's a Saint Francis, pure and simple! He's always in a state of grace and it just keeps on pursuing him! Goddamn it! Another night's sleep down the drain!"

*

Vladimír seemed to be forever starting over again, like a new immigrant or a child. When we'd go to a soccer match, he'd first stare in wonder, then he'd start asking naive questions. Which uniforms were Slavia's, and which were the visitors'? He'd ask what an offside was, what a goal was, what an "out of play" was, what a foul was. When the fans within earshot would lose patience and start yelling at him, Vladimír would declare that a game like soccer was the perfect image of a magnetic force field, and he was happiest when the teams were evenly matched because that was what a proper work of art should be, a balanced ebb and flow of opposites. He'd claim you could draw the lines of force delineating the movements of the attackers and the tactics of the defenders. But what excited him most was when the ball was in play and both teams were galvanized into action. To Vladimír, the most beautiful thing about soccer was when the players surged forward and flowed into a vacuum, when one team moved in to score against the other. In the end, he came to see soccer as a game resembling what happens at the entrance to a pub, which has to withstand the pressure of ten people trying to exit the pub while another ten people are trying to force their way in.

Once we went to the Slavoj VIII club, which was hosting a tournament of deaf-mute teams. The game had an extra balletic and kinetic quality to it. With every foul, the players tried, through gestures, to explain to the referee what had happened, how they felt wronged, and it all took place as if in a beautiful silent movie, through pantomime and elements of dance. All that night, and for a long time thereafter, Vladimír talked about the connection between soccer and Explosionalist graphics, and one evening, at the King Václav pub, ladies decked out in their best gowns and hairdos kept coming in, along with former soccer players from Meteor and the Libeň Sports Club and Čechie Karlín. They were all awaiting the appearance of a once handsome, raven-haired soccer player who lived in the Jewish quarter of Libeň and who, when he arrived, would turn his chair around, sit down, and tell stories about his soccer exploits. When Vladimír spoke about the one match he had attended in the past three months, he astonished everyone with his vivid portrayal of the players and his wonderful insights into key moments in the match. After he'd finished, a round of bracing liqueurs was served to the ladies, and Vladimír got a large cognac for his gripping account, and the former players winked knowingly at each other because even if they thought Vladimír quite mad, his enthralling descriptions of the game allowed them to see it from another angle altogether.

*

To Vladimír, the normal world was a sanatorium, a world of striving citizens, longing for consumer goods and seeing themselves in terms of statistical averages. When he was feeling depressed to the point of madness, he accepted the game of this world. It gave him a chance to rest and renew his strength. He would turn down the wick of his overheated lamp to avoid cracking the glass chimney. He'd do the shopping, go to the movies, and he'd even taken up fishing. He became a completely different person, and so, even though he looked upon consumer society as if from a satellite circling the earth, he sometimes liked to play at being a participant, just as children love going to a curiosity museum, to a hall of mirrors, the Planetarium, or the Julius Fučík amusement park. Thus it might be said that the limiting selfishness of ordinary people spurred him on to greater heights. But he was not like them. He dressed like them, and went to work like them, and held in contempt that Neitzschean *Allzumenschlichkeit*, that all too human quality, so that by using the extension ladder of his imagination, he could run it up as far as it would go and climb to the top rung, into the beautiful, stormy clouds.

*

When Vladimír married Tekla, they at first discussed whether she should study aesthetics, or learn languages, or go to a graphic arts school. Tekla ended up working in the same place as Vladimír. She learned how to operate a lathe, wore overalls with big braces and, with her beautiful breasts, she became the darling of the factory. After each shift, Vladimír liked to sit in the women's section under the big clock and, as they emerged from the showers, he would engage them in a conversation about his marital life, and in such detail that the women would blush to the roots of their hair. Vladimír deeply regretted that Tekla had to shower in the factory. Before she started working there, Vladimír would bathe her himself in a washtub. To please her, he'd walk naked in front of her with a splendid erection. When the ladies worried that Vladimír might be wearing himself out that way, he reassured them that he did this, and other things, in front of his wife for her own pleasure. Most of all, Vladimír enjoyed sitting with a lesbian worker who liked to shower with Tekla, and so Vladimír, who admired his wife's body, would sit in quiet conversation with the lesbian, sharing experiences and observations with her, and even though they were of different sexual persuasions, they were always in agreement. They whispered so loudly, however, that the other women workers were even more embarrassed, though they looked on Vladimír with admiration, each one wishing she had a man at home as deeply in love as Vladimír was.

When Egon Bondy heard about this, he shouted: "You're

doing it on purpose again! That dyke was whispering to Vladimír so I'd never know what they were talking about. Vladimír, goddamn it! I always thought I was the specialist in that area, because I took guidance from the old Gnostics, who believed that sexual deviance was the gateway to the spiritual life. So is Vladimír mocking me, even in his factory? With Vladimír, it just never, ever ends."

I whispered to Egon: "I remember, once, in the Embankment of Eternity, Vladimír stuck a Christmas tree candle so deeply up his nose that ..."

Egon Bondy roared: "Fucking hell! A Christmas tree candle, and he stuck it up his nose?"

"Up his nose ..." I replied.

Egon Bondy ran and kicked the air, then grabbed his knee: "It's given me a cramp in my leg, but why up his nose, for fuck's sake?"

"To give himself the tactile sensation of homosexual penetration," I replied. "I had to extract it with a pair of pliers. It's a good thing the wick was still intact."

And Egon Bondy knocked me down and tickled my face with his chin and cried out: "You two are not paying attention, and I will kill, kill, kill!" Then he pushed me away and looked up at the ceiling and cried out ecstatically to the heavens: "This is Paris, right here! In Prague! In Libeň! It's Galicia. Vladimír is the son of the rabbi of Belz. Absolute and pure insanity!"

*

Once, a couple of weeks after Vladimír and Tekla got married, Bondy decided we should visit them. I said: "In that case, we have to look in on them in Na Žertvách Street. He's living in a basement where Jiří Šmejkal lives. Šmejkal's just finished whitewashing the place."

It was evening when we arrived at the door. The shutters were drawn, but not completely, so through a small crack you could see Vladimír pacing up and down in the neon light, his golden curls ablaze as always. It was beautiful: Vladimír's torso, as though he were standing in a grave, flickered in and out of sight an arm's length away. He was talking as he paced rapidly up and down the long basement room. Then Tekla appeared, her beauty very much that of a woman of aristocratic blood, and she paced alongside Vladimír, trying to explain something to him as he became more and more agitated. The walls, freshly whitewashed, were dazzling, and Vladimír and Tekla moved back and forth, gesticulating. Vladimír seemed to be reproaching her for something, Tekla defended herself, and the cellar was as charged with static as a Leyden jar.

Egon Bondy, squatting in front of the window, exhaled and hissed: "Fucking hell, he's a real piece of work, that Vladimír. This is going to end in a catastrophe!" And he was right. Vladimír, beautiful in his wrath and his indignation, bellowed and shot bolts of lightning at Tekla, who knelt in front of him, but each time, Vladimír would pull her roughly to her feet and then set off pacing again, with her scurrying to keep up.

I turned away and there, across the railway tracks, in the row of two-story houses on the other side of Na Žertvách Street, I could see a lighted window open on the second floor and through it, under a bare light bulb, a half-finished portrait of a naked woman reclining on an antique canapé and the artist who was working on it, his back to the street, looking toward the other end of the room, where there was a second window, obscured by a decorative iron shutter. The artist would jab his paintbrush at the canvas with enormous passion, giving vent to the emotions inspired in him by female flesh.

"Bondy, look," I said, taking him by the shoulder, but at that very moment a steam locomotive rumbled across Na Žertvách, belching out clouds of dense white smoke that not only obscured the facades of the buildings opposite, but enveloped us as well. When the train had passed and the smoke cleared, Egon Bondy looked through the open window at the artist's back, and watched his head turn away from the canvas and back again to focus on his portrait of a woman who lay somewhere out of sight in a quiet corner of the room, her legs spread wide. Bondy placed an uncomprehending finger against his lips, then turned back and looked through the crack in the shutters at Vladimír who, at the height of his excitement, had brought in a bucket of creosote into which he dipped his brush and, with powerful strokes, was laying down thick black streaks and splattering gobs of creosote onto the white wall, surrendering to the rhythm of his Explosionalistic passion. Eventually he calmed down, but as he worked, he disappeared from our field of vision, though we could still hear the brush periodically knocking against the side of the bucket. Then Tekla appeared, as much of her as we could see through the gap. She stood watching Vladimír as he worked, her anger and fear seemed to have vanished, at least as far as we could tell.

Egon waited by the second basement window until Vladimír reappeared. The gap in the shutters here was wider, so we ran from one window to the other, watching Tekla, who was now speaking, gesturing, offering Vladimír advice, encouraging him. So it was I who caught sight of Vladimír's long shadow and his maniacal work, work that destroyed Jiří Šmejkal's basement flat. His shadow drew close, then moved on, then his hand appeared, and finally, the rest of him. Egon Bondy said: "Doctor, what we're seeing here is the essence of true obscenity, the revelation of a mystery. It's magnificent! When I consult Zbyněk Fišer about this ..."

An electric current passed through Vladimír's body, and he paced off three meters, and now we could see all of him, excited, focused, his bright face glowing in anticipation of the approaching climax. The spots and splatters and the abrupt, explosive rhythms of the brush dipped in the bucket of creosote were resplendent, and just as he had once dreamed of running a creosote-covered bathroom wall through his rotogravure press, he was now creating a creosote-covered wall, giving vent to a suffering whose essence we did not know.

We had barely managed to turn around when we saw the painter across the road straighten up and step back to reveal the portrait, clumps of glowing female flesh adorned with patches of horsehair in the crotch and the armpits and the hair on her head aflame in full color, and as powerful as that portrait was, by the same degree the painter now wilted and slumped in his chair, his arms draped over his knees. A woman's hand reached out, pulled a porcelain knob, venetian blinds crashed down, and the hand vanished from sight.

Once Vladimír had smeared every wall in that enormous cellar, he moved away slowly, as though his feet were sticking in the thickening creosote. It took time for him to walk from the gap in the second window back to the first. He was also six inches shorter and bent over, and the lines around his mouth sagged. Tekla walked casually behind him and they crossed the corridor into the next room, which they called the office, and the cellar went dark.

Egon Bondy turned around, and the lights in the second-floor window across the street went out. He was silent, reached out his arm, and offered me his dainty, feminine hand so I'd feel his trembling fingers. He merely nodded and a strand of hair fell across his forehead, making him look like a hungover Dionysus ...

The next day Tekla ran over and stood in our courtyard, wringing her hands. "Doctor, Doctor," she called out, "please, come at once. Vladimír's gone mad."

I grabbed my coat and on the way, tried to pry out of her what was going on, but all she could do was wring her hands. When I went down into the cellar, the shutters were still closed and the acrid smell of flickering light bulbs permeated the dank air. Vladimír lay on a bed by the wall, splattered and smeared with shiny creosote, and the entire cellar was like an ancient diorama full of black tree trunks, Vladimír's head covered with ugly bruises and welts that had swollen ominously, some of them protruding like horns. "For the love of God, Vladimír," I said, "what's wrong with you?"

He got up and pounded his head violently against the wall over and over, rattling his brain and leaving fragments of plaster and creosote embedded in his forehead. I lunged forward and pulled him away from the wall, but he knocked me down with maniacal strength and Tekla jumped in to separate us but he shook us both off as though we were children and resumed pounding his head against the wall. We pulled him away again and dragged him into the middle of the room, but he pulled us both back to the wall as though we weighed no more than the clothes we had on and, rising to his feet, he smashed his head against the wall so hard we could feel the shock waves passing through our arms. And with one final blow, he collapsed and we carried him to the bed.

I laid my hand on his forehead and could feel the lumps on his bruised and battered skull. Tekla soaked towels in water and we took turns applying them to his head and as Tekla carried the compresses in from the tap in the corridor, she left a sparkling trail of water drops behind her. I asked her to fetch some aluminum acetate, a lot of cotton batten and bandages, then watched as she ran up the stairs and stepped into the street, and through the gap in the shutters I could see her feet as she hurried past the window.

Vladimír came to. "Vladimír," I said, "what have you done to yourself? Why did you hurt yourself? Why?"

Vladimír turned his head in profile against the pillow and, with tears running down his cheeks, he whispered: "She told me about the boys that had her and then left her, and she lay there in the field and in her anguish ate little mounds of soft earth, molehills ... I was so moved ... I wanted to comfort her ... take all the evil upon myself ... ease her pain ... I wanted her to see I'd do anything for her ... and give her some joy, something to remember ... so she'd know I belong to a proud generation that takes life seriously ... Do you see?"

It was quiet for a while, and you could hear footfalls on the sidewalk, some quick, some slow, according to how each person bore his or her own lot in life past Vladimír's cellar ...

Then the outer door flew open and Tekla was back, her arms full of bandages and packages of cotton batten, and I saw how, when she came to the door leading to the basement room, she got her bearings as quickly as a rat, raised her leg and pressed the door handle with the sole of her shoe, opened it, entered the room, and bumped the door shut with her behind. We bandaged Vladimír up, having first dusted his wounds with a disinfectant powder, then cleansed them with cotton batten soaked in aluminum acetate. As I was leaving, I paused at the top of the stairs and looked back, bending down so I could see the bed. Tekla was sitting at the head of it, plumping the pillow and arranging the corners under Vladimír's head, which was turned toward her, watching her fingers with blissful eyes.

"Everything good now?" I asked.

"It's good," Tekla replied, and Vladimír smiled, then quietly laughed his victorious laugh.

*

I have seen two people in my life with the imprint of God's thumb on their foreheads. Vladimír, and Egon Bondy. Two jewels of materialist thought, two Christs in the guise of Lenin, two romantics who had the good fortune, at the age of twenty-five, to explore the retinal terrain of a university library ...

*

Vladimír and I were fond of the World Cafeteria because Mrs. Vlaštovková was always cheerful and her beer was always the best. But when we heard the story of how the cafeteria, the shopping complex, the restaurant, and the World Cinema came to be, we started going to all the movies.

In a part of Libeň they call the Jewish Quarter, there had once been an estate owned by a Mr. Svět – Mr. World. He thought about it, and concluded that his name wasn't entirely accidental. So he sold everything he owned, borrowed more money, and built the World complex. The premiere presentation at the cinema was an American blockbuster called *Noah's Ark*. But what Mr. Svĕt hadn't counted on was groundwater fed by the nearby Vltava River. While the rain was sheeting down on the screen and the ark was sailing on through the downpour, the groundwater from the Vltava seeped into the cinema and the audience found themselves up to their ankles in water while the movie played on to the end. The estate owner, Mr. Svĕt, lost a million crowns on the cinema. He shot himself. And now, during every screening, you can hear the sump pumps working away in the basement. Above the restaurant there's a wrought-iron globe and a sign: THE WORLD.

When Vladimír took Egon Bondy to the World Cinema and Bondy heard the pumps and the story of the place, he shouted out loud: "Jebem ti boga tryskovego! – Fuck it! There are three hundred cinemas in Prague, and this is the one Vladimír goes to? Phooey, phooey!" and he spat on the floor and carried on, just as the newsreel was showing the ceremonial arrival of a Soviet statesman in Prague. The attendants brought the lights up and ushered Bondy out, claiming his outburst could have untold consequences for the whole world.

*

One morning we were drinking Pilsner in the restaurant U Slovanské Lípy. Later, sitting in the sun in the beer garden, we looked up at the surrounding balcony and there was St. John of Nepomuk, large as life. The fellows at our table were having a boorish conversation: "You should have seen the size of the knockers on her. A butcher's dog could have grabbed them and wrapped them round his neck." "Gentlemen, having sex with your wife after five years of marriage ought to be treated as incest and land you in jail."

We took our glasses and retreated to the taproom. A young man with a bandage around his eyes sat down beside us. To take a drink, he had to tilt his head back as though gargling. "It's nothing," he said dismissively, but after two beers he opened up: "I'm a welder and I have arc eye." Then he went on about a girl he'd known. "It's a summer night. My hand's on her panties and the elastic's broken. I wilted, and that was it for me."

The remark triggered in Vladimír memories of Tekla. "My strength is in my failures," he said. "Sometimes the pressure inside my head is so so strong I need a relief valve. What can I do? She ran away ... I'm wearing her panties. It's the second pair. I tore the first one up, put them in an envelope. And now look, I'm wearing her sweater. It's hardly a sweater anymore, just a mass of threads. She wanted money and that's why she's gone, and here I am, falling apart. If she ever gives me the slightest encouragement, I'll write her letters with my penis."

By now Vladimír was shouting. He ran into the garden and stood in the courtyard in the sun with his back to the wall, tears running down his cheeks. He didn't bother wiping them away. I paid up and we walked along the busy street and people probably thought Vladimír's mother, or maybe his child, had just died. We started to cross the street on a red light but the traffic cop waved us through with his striped nightstick, indicating that he understood, and he even held up traffic for us as we crossed the intersection like an ambulance, like cop cars on their way to a fire or a catastrophic car accident.

We walked all the way to Libeň, to the King George, where

Vladimír wiped away his tears and we sat down beside a drunken carpenter from Kotlaska Street who was asleep with his head on the table. Then a young man with a large bald spot walked in and dropped a sack full of young pigeons on the table and the squabs were struggling to get to their feet, then falling down again, and the young man slapped the bag and they calmed down, or more likely simply fell over. Someone at the next table was just finishing his side of a conversation: "So gentleman, Jaroslav Hašek was a hotshot. By the time he turned forty, he'd written a novel and six hundred stories. Has anyone ever topped that?"

The drunken carpenter raised his head and said, "I've made six hundred sideboards in my life. And that son of a bitch Hašek? The wife read his stuff and it made her so wild she ran off on me. Hašek wrecked my marriage." Before sinking back down to the table again, the drunk planted his elbows on the tablecloth and, to add weight to his words, brought his fist down hard on the bag where the squabs were still struggling to find their feet. A patch of blood seeped into the white tablecloth. The handsome young bald man heaved a sigh of satisfaction. "Saves me having to wring their necks," he said.

Vladimír got to his feet, his face radiant: "Doctor, I'm a bum. Will you buy me ten packets of paper? Will you buy me paints? As many as I need? Let's go." And he pointed at the spot left by the crushed pigeons and at the drunk and then, on his way out the door, he shouted: "Reality is way ahead of me. I'll try to catch up this evening."

*

Vladimír's life resembled the work of a human heart that could also think. From all the things that happened to him, he would select and embrace only what suited him, not every experience, just the ones that contained creative feelings and ideas. He could tell which ones by a trembling and tingling throughout his entire being, a set of signals that had been part of him since childhood, something present at the very beginning of life, a plasma, a liquid seed that, through all the umbilical cords, ultimately returns to the smooth, navel-less belly of the Ur-mother, Eve. Vladimír's creative work was a *regressus ad originem*. Through tactile experiences, he allowed himself to be drawn back into the maternal womb and, pulling one vagina after another over his head like a sweater, he would, like Goethe, get back to the Great Mother. Vladimír's return, however, his *regressus ad originem*, was at the same time a *progressus ad futurum*. The circle was completed, the first day of Creation touched the end of days ... eternity.

*

Vladimír's erections and ejaculations were transcendental. His semen could impregnate a virgin while leaving her virginity intact. It was the injection of fuel directly to the spark plugs without first passing through the carburetor. The only question was: how resistant was the material. The work was the child of an idea. Such benevolence! The Catholic God, too, is able to act directly, without a causal nexus, without a carburetor. Zap! And that's how it is, and it's as rock solid as the Helvetic faith! Anna, Hea, Mulge. Father, Son, and Holy Ghost. The immaculate conception of the Virgin Mary, unmediated, through the power of the Spirit alone.

That was how it was with Vladimír. Anointing himself with his own semen as he worked, he applied it as well to the plates of the rotogravure press, gripping the device in a hammerlock or a full nelson, anointing everything with semen, even the newborn creation that passed through the birth canal of the printing press and emerged on the other side as a lithograph. Lightning taking the shortest route to the ground.

And so what began as extreme subjectivity ended in objectivization, a self-contained world in which Vladimír had been anarchically addressed by the motion of matter within matter, and through his lithographs, he launched himself into a space that defies analysis. Through relative freedom, he arrived at a state of absolute unfreedom no longer requiring explanation or justification, a state in which one is what one is. A oneness of the music of the spheres with stuff scattered about on the ground. Absolute play; *fruitio dei*, the enjoyment of God; the monad of monads, *ens realissimum*, the most real being, *Ding an sich selbst*, the cave in which ideas, not just their shadows, are visible. Thus he took a step beyond, into a place and a purpose that transcends us. Vladimír, as the firstborn son of God, addressed matter and action and reestablished drama as the active expression of love for the Universe and for Man.

*

Vladimír often had me tell him two stories that, for reasons I could not fathom, excited him. One was about Sep Bruml, who had a friend he enjoyed talking to so much that in the course of a single conversation they would cross the Libeň Bridge together several times. Mr. Bruml would take the elevator with him and escort him right to his door, but since the conversation was far from over, they would take the elevator back down again and walk back across the bridge, then again take the elevator to Mr.

Bruml's door, but as Mr. Bruml was slipping the key into the lock, they realized the conversation wasn't over yet, so they'd go back down the elevator again and Mr. Bruml would walk across to Libeň with his friend . . .

But the most beautiful story of all, in Vladimír's mind, was the legend of the friendship between Mr. Kocourek, the head teacher from Velenka, and Mr. Talacko, the head teacher from Semice. When they had finished drinking their beer in the pubs, they would take turns walking each other home through the starry night, and each time, they determined there was still more to be said about the problem of educating the young, so they would turn around and walk together from one gate back to the other one three kilometers away. In the summer months, they would walk back and forth until dawn and it was only because they were exhausted that the two teachers felt compelled to go to bed. When Mr. Talacko traveled to Prague from Poříčany, the two friends would agree to meet in Chrast, in Mandršejt, or in Mans, to discuss what was new. There was always so much new to talk about that when they reached Semice, the teacher would put his briefcase away and walk with his friend back to Velenka.

When Vladimír heard the story, he was moved and as he followed the journey of those two teachers in his mind, he said they must have been very happy. Then I told him something I had learned only recently, that Mr. Kocourek's daughter had fallen in love with a young man from Mandršejt, but the head teacher disapproved of their love and the young man shot himself in the head and the girl placed her handkerchief under his bleeding head, then jumped into the Labe River near Přívlaky.

When Vladimír heard this, he stared into the very heart of

that unhappy love and said: "I've always wanted a friendship like that. Did those two friends go on walking each other home after what happened?"

I told him I'd heard they did. Even after they retired, they often walked back and forth, from the gate in Velenka to the gate in Semice and back again, and when they were no longer up to it, they wrote each other every day, with messages and news of themselves.

Vladimír and I never again talked about those stories, and perhaps we'd even forgotten them, yet when we had something to talk about, Vladimír would walk with me to Libeň and then, from the Embankment of Eternity, we'd walk back and stand on Kostnické Square in front of his building, Vladimír would stick his key into the lock, but then, thinking it over, he would remove the key and walk with me, by way of Pražačka, back to the Embankment of Eternity, as the two teachers, Talacko and Kocourek, hovered over us like clouds in a baroque fresco.

*

Back then, after Vladimír left his mother and moved to the Old Town and from there to Libeň, and then back again to his mother's place, entangled in the umbilical cord, not of an Oedipal complex, but of a maternal complex in which the mother was a symbol of creativity, we'd walk each other back and forth, pondering the fact that, as sons of absentee fathers, neither of us suffered from a paternal complex. It was a privileged state to be in, to be able to disregard one's father, one's only complex a filial complex, that is, to have only oneself as a model, yet never to become a model to oneself unless the essence of that model is contempt for models. In other words, it was our mission to live at the expense of ourselves and the Universe, to wage a constant war with ourselves, to conclude a peace that would never be concluded, to be in a constant state of creative tension and intoxication.

When Egon Bondy heard about these conversations, he shouted: "I refuse to waste my time getting angry at Vladimír. I'll simply kill him and that will be the end of it. What he's saying is exactly what I'm living through as a left-wing Marxist, a state of permanent revolution, of permanent revolt against my father, because so far every murdered father has been replaced by a son, and when that son becomes a father, he can expect to be murdered in turn. But damn it all! We're just sons, nothing more. Long live permanent revolution!"

*

One morning in Libeň, when we were still half-asleep, we got a terrible fright. Vladimír's foot had swollen so badly he couldn't get his shoe on. So he put on a pair of slippers and that afternoon we set off to the local clinic, to see Dr. Adam.

When we stepped into his office, Vladimír leaning against me for support, Dr. Adam, looking singularly human with his pince-nez and his shaven head, said: "So, my two silly lads, you got plastered, is that it? Let's have a look." And Vladimír stretched out his leg and the doctor examined his painful, swollen foot. Then he walked across the room, opened his office door and said, in a loud, good-natured voice so everyone in the packed waiting room could hear: "Get out of my clinic, silly boy, before I kick you down the stairs and all the way to Palmovka!" We left in a hurry while Dr. Adam explained to the waiting room and to our retreating backs: "That stupid fellow was so drunk he put three socks on one foot!"

*

Vladimír and I liked going to a dive bar called the Village, where they served only hard liquor. It wasn't just because we liked drinking from their oddly-shaped shot glasses, but mostly because the place had no windows and Vladimír loved the gloom, especially when the weather outside was sunny and the only light came in through the glass door. As time went on, we took to arriving at the Village fifteen minutes before the proprietor opened up, lifting the iron barrier and opening the heavy oaken doors shaped like a pair of angels' wings. In that quarter of an hour, an old woman would show up holding a tin cup. She'd sit down on the step and wait, and then five minutes before opening time she'd grow impatient, walk up to the gate and put her ear against it, listening anxiously for signs of life. When she heard noises inside, she'd gently tap the tin cup against the iron barrier as if she were trapped at the bottom of a mine, alerting the rescuers to her location. When the door finally opened, she was the first to rush inside, where she ordered a double shot of rye and, still standing at the bar, began sipping it as tears of relief streamed down her cheeks. Then she'd buy enough to fill her cup, take a sip from it on the way out and carry the cup home, sprightly, alert, and cheerful.

"How old is she?" Vladimír asked the proprietor.

The proprietor rinsed out our glasses, held them up to the light, and poured us another round. "Seventy-six, and she'll be back again this evening."

"Doctor," Vladimír said, "let's drink a toast to the lady's health. If she has a world-class doctor when she's in her nineties, she'll last till she's a hundred and thirty. People like her have immortal innards."

"Exactly," said the proprietor, pouring himself a glass of rye and adding: "Me, when I see the old bag get such a kick out of drinking from her tin cup, I get an irresistible urge to pour myself a drink as well." And he raised the shot glass, which sparkled like a chandelier of Venetian glass, clicked his heels together, and tossed it back.

Vladimír and I poured a few drops of ouzo into our hands, rubbed it on our faces and hair, then carefully massaged it into the backs of our necks. "It's good for the vertebrae," Vladimír said, and redolent of anise, we stepped out into the sunlight and walked three doors down to Ferka's for a beer, just for the exercise.

*

Vladimír and I would go to Hausman's in our slippers, because it was just around the corner. I had brought a bicycle to Prague from Nymburk, and one day, we borrowed a second bicycle, put an alarm clock into a briefcase, one of those horrible twin-bell Roskopfs that were so loud it could rouse people several blocks away, and we set off on an outing to Hausman's. We'd scarcely made it past the building next door, where patented funeral lights were made, when we ran into Egon Bondy.

"I'll be buggered," Egon said. "Vladimír, what are you doing on a bicycle? Where are you off to?"

"Egon," I said, "jump on behind, or sit on the crossbar. We're doing this for our health."

Bondy was in a good mood, so he jumped on behind me and we turned into Ludmila Street and rode the bicycles into the entrance passage, parked them against the wall, and ordered beer. Mr. Vanista was alarmed: "What's with those bikes in the passageway? Where are you off to?"

"The doctor recommended we go bike riding," I replied.

"So where have you come from?" Mr. Vanista asked.

"From Fiala's. From home!"

"There goes today, down the shitter!" Mr. Vanista shouted.

Suddenly, out in the passageway, the Austrian Roskop alarm clock in the briefcase went off. Mr. Vanista listened for a moment. He was startled, and so was Bondy. "What is this, some kind of alert?" he shouted. "A fire alarm? What the fuck! Goddamn it! What is it?"

Mr. Vanista ran outside, because the alarm clock was vibrating so violently that it had knocked the bicycles over and the handlebars had gouged the plaster. He stood holding the briefcase with the alarm clock clanging as though it contained a bomb or some other devilish device. Vladimír calmly opened the briefcase, extracted the still-ringing clock, and placed it on the bar. The two bell hammers were vibrating so vigorously the clock moved of its own accord along the zinc surface. Mr. Vanista tossed the clock into the sink where it went on ringing, even underwater, though it now sounded like a muted flugelhorn. But it kept on ringing, and Mr. Vanista laughed till the tears came. "What an amazing machine," he said. "Chalk another one up for old Austria."

When the clock finally stopped ringing, I fished it dripping out of the sink, rewound it, and then set the alarm hand a little further ahead. The alarm went off again, louder and more urgently than before, and we put the clock back in the brief-case, paid up, and trundled the bicycles into the street. Bondy jumped on behind, and we set off on our invigorating ride home, one block away, where Egon gave us a beautiful lecture on how, if there is no God, and no ideas that have any direct impact anymore, the hero of modern times, to achieve recognition, must necessarily be a psychopath.

*

One morning Vladimír and I were walking through Karlín, and as we were passing the Green Tree pub, we were surprised to see two sleighs parked outside, because it was summer. So we went inside. There, on a wobbly ladder, stood a housepainter, Mr. Nejedlo, who lived on the third floor above the Vanistas and who, like Vladimír, suffered from asphyxiophilia. Once every three months, he would get very drunk and then strangle himself on the door handle inside his flat while his wife was outside on the courtyard walkway. She would find him just in time and release him.

Mr. Nejedlo had beautiful brown doe-like eyes, and he was fond of us. The taproom counter and the beer taps were covered with a sheet spattered with paint, and the shelves were covered with sheets, as well, but there were two old men sitting at a table, where they had cleared a small space for themselves and they were waiting for the pub to start serving beer in a couple of hours. They were both toothless, and because it was summer they were wearing only trousers and slippers, nor had they bothered to do up their flies. They each had two slices of bread wrapped in newspaper in front of them. They were regulars who'd been dying for a drink since the place had closed for painting two days before, and they could think of nothing better to do than sit there, staring at the beer taps under the sheets.

"Where are you off to?" Mr. Nejedlo asked, and we told him nowhere in particular. He yelled into the kitchen and the pubkeeper emerged and brought us two bottles of beer. The old men wrung their hands imploringly, so he brought them beer as well. We sat there with the two old men and the pubkeeper got into the mood and brought out more beer and Mr. Nejedlo went on teetering on his wobbly ladder, spattering the old men, and us, with paint. The more spattered we became, the more voluble Vladimír grew and the more he talked, the deeper into detail he went about how, ever since he was in art school, he liked to strangle himself. I kicked him under the table but Mr. Nejedlo, teetering back and forth on his ladder like a metronome, fixed his big doe eyes on us while the paint-spattered old men went to relieve themselves and came back, still unbuttoned. They had both been trained as blacksmiths, both had retired from the trade on the same day, and both were widowers. They would spread two slices of bread with pork fat each day, put it on the sleighs, and pull the sleighs home again at night.

"That's how it should be," said Vladimír when he heard their stories.

Later, when we'd said goodbye to Mr. Nejedlo, Vladimír remarked the painter had eyes as beautiful as an art nouveau poster girl, as anyone in the entire Jugendstil canon.

Three days later, Mr. Vanista invited us to a funeral. The pubkeepers' association, Hostimil, was laying one of its members to rest, and Mr. Vanista, who had a voice almost as beautiful as Beniamino Gigli's, had been asked to sing. Afterward, we went to the funeral reception at the Hotel Splendid, and when it was over Mr. Vanista invited us back to his pub where he promised to play us a recording of himself singing "Adio mare," and to go with it, he'd break open a fresh barrel of beer.

When we arrived at Ludmila Street by taxi, the main entrance to the building was wide open, though by now it was close to midnight. Mr. Vanista leaped out of the taxi and shouted: "What the hell is going on, leaving the place open like this? I'll be robbed blind!" As he was about to lock the door, some men came down the stairs carrying a black coffin, their thin legs bending under the weight. Vladimír stared at the sight with mounting horror. A hearse appeared out of the night shadows and the shiny coffin was slid into it, while down the stairs came the building superintendent, Mrs. Valečková, her eyes still lined with soot from her day job delivering coal. She walked a little unsteadily to the main door, kicked one half of it shut with her foot, then said to Mr. Vanista: "Lad'a, I feel like I've been ripped open ... D'you know who that was they carried out? Nejedlo, the housepainter. He hung himself on the door handle ... He thought Růža, his wife, was coming, but I got talking to her and she had her hand on the door handle, and on the other side of it ... he was hanging by his neck. If I'd only known ..." Mrs. Valečková said, her hands as big as hockey gloves.

"Doctor," Vladimír whispered, "if I were to shoot myself, would you lay a handkerchief under my head?"

*

Once, Egon Bondy decided to favor us with a reading of one of his stories. To mark the occasion he bought a beautiful red polka-dot tie, and then he proposed that he and Vladimír go for two buckets of beer to steady his nerves before the reading. First they brought in two buckets from Lišeks, then two more from the Old Post Office. Finally, Bondy decided they should go to Hausman's for another two because he still didn't feel quite up to reading his stories, his artifacts, as he called them, with the proper élan. But when they got to Hausman's, it was closed. Egon Bondy knocked on the door with one fist, then with both, then he and Vladimír banged their tin pails against the glass panels in the door, then they listened, but still Mr. Vanista didn't come to open up.

"Goddamn it!" Bondy yelled. "Hey you, bartender! Get the hell out of bed! Poets have come for beer!" And with one blow from his tin pail, he smashed in the panel and the shattered glass crashed onto the cement floor. "Hey there!" Bondy roared, "the pride of the nation have come for beer and you're in there sawing logs!" He bent down to look into the bar through the broken window, and the door burst open and Mr. Vanista flew out in his underpants, an angry, hundred-kilogram pubkeeper with a club in his hand. However, when he saw Vladimír, whom he liked, he froze with his arm aloft, holding the shiny thing, which was really a bull's penis reinforced with steel rods.

"How dare you!" shouted Egon Bondy, while Vladimír wrung his hands. Bondy kept on: "What kind of barman are you, raising your hand against poets?"

"Who'll pay for this broken window?" Mr. Vanista yelled. "Who? Who? Who? Who?"

"Give us two pails of beer at once!" Egon Bondy retorted. "Beer for poets!" he ordered.

Mr. Vanista raised the club again, but Vladimír implored him with his eyes to back down.

"Ah, so that's your game!" said Egon cockily. "Do you know who I am? Egon Bondy, the poet."

And Mr. Vanista shot back: "You can kiss my ass. Who's going to pay for that window? Poet or not, I'll give you a punch in the teeth!"

"Who, me?" Bondy roared, "Punch a poet? When I tell Zbyněk Fišer, the philosopher, about this, he'll punch you in the face!"

I ran up and stayed a blow from the bull's penis. "Lad'a," I said, "I'll pay for everything. He's a real poet, can't you tell?"

Mr. Vanista relented, the tension in his flushed neck eased, the arm holding the club dropped, and he laughed. "You know what, Doctor? Of course he's a poet. I could tell as soon as he broke the window. So come on in, boys. A poet, you say? He looks a bit nervous, but if anyone has a right to be nervous these days, it's poets, am I right?"

And so, back at the Embankment of Eternity, Egon Bondy read us a beautiful story about a man called Antonín, who escaped on foot across the border into Bavaria, and about the many things that happened to him in the course of twenty-four hours, and after all his tribulations, Antonín thought that the cottage he saw ahead of him was of Bavarian construction but when he reached it, he saw that it was the same cottage from which, that very day, he had set out on his illicit journey across the border.

Egon Bondy was worried to death that all the pubs were about to close and we'd suffer from thirst, so he woke up the woman who lived on the ground floor where there used to be a laundry, and he borrowed a ewer and a pail from her and the three of us took all our containers and bought enough beer to fill them all. After we had polished it off, Egon Bondy stood stiffly with his head erect as though his spine were in a cast. He consented to have us walk him to the tram stop, and while we were waiting for the tram, Bondy fell backward, crashing into a storefront shutter, then slumping to the sidewalk, his head bumping along the corrugated metal.

It so happened that behind the shutter were offices of the civilian police, and two uniformed officers and a sergeant, his tunic unbuttoned, ran out onto the street. Bondy was lying there on his back and they helped him sit up, while all thirty pages of the story of Antonín and his illicit border crossing lay scattered over the ground like spent lottery tickets.

Vladimír and I were horrified and kept quiet, but Egon Bondy cried, "Sergeant, can't you see? For God's sake, pick up my pages, and be quick about it or the streetcar will run them over, goddamn it!"

The young police officers gathered up the pages that told the story of Antonín, who had tried to escape to Bavaria, in enemy territory, and as they were handing him back the pages, the sergeant glanced at the text, then lingered over an entire page, nodding, and when the almost empty streetcar slowed to a stop, he gave a signal with his chin and the two young officers helped Egon Bondy into the tram and as Bondy rode off, clutching the pages the sergeant had handed him, he sang out: "Nobody knows, not even the narcs, that I'm well to the left of Karl Marx . . ."

"I've no doubt," the sergeant said forlornly, and he waved his hand dismissively and the two young policemen went back into their warm office. The old sergeant paused on the top step, turned, and said to us, because we were looking downcast: "A good thing no one from the state police read that stuff. Good night." And he pulled the shutter down with a thunderous racket.

"All the same," Vladimír said, "Egon Bondy is quite an affable and lively young lad. He gave us a rather pleasant evening. Just now though, I'm about to throw up. Would you care to join me, Doctor?"

*

When Vladimír got married a second time, in Český Krumlov, he asked me to be his best man. I was in for a surprise. I set out in my car but I couldn't get out of Prague, neither through the city center, nor by using back routes, because the fraternal armies had arrived with their tanks to liquidate a nonexistent problem. So I returned home and then went to see an exhibition of modern American art in the Waldstein Riding School. I knocked on the gate, but the show had been postponed because the armies had arrived. When Egon Bondy heard about this, he shouted: "Goddamn it! That Vladimír! Will I ever have the good fortune to have so many armies set in motion because I'm getting married? The only thing in my life to rival that, Doctor, was when you delivered my greetings to Rudi Dutschke, and you went into his apartment building just as they were carrying him out after he was shot in the head. But setting five armies in motion just to stop a wedding? That's something I'll never be able to fathom. And why?

Because Vladimír has always attracted great events and great misfortune. That's how it is. Goddamn it! What amazing luck the man has!"

*

We were sitting with friends just opposite the bar at the Tomcat. Vladimír was sitting next to the poet Marysko, who had come to the Embankment of Eternity in the nineteen fifties with three suitcases and lived with us, and because he was always cold, he slept behind the kitchen stove, which we pulled out from the wall to accommodate him. Vladimír had often wanted to usher Marysko out of this world because whenever they meet, he'd ask Vladimír the same question: "Do you know how to draw a hand?" and each time, Vladimír would get terribly upset. That day, however, when Marysko asked Vladimír if he knew how to draw a hand, Vladimír merely smiled.

We were having a good time at the Tomcat with friends, and the bartender, Mr. Čihák, who had come here from the Golden Tiger, was drawing his amazing glasses of beer topped with creamy foam, when a hand swept aside the red draft curtain by the door and the film director Miloš Forman, entered the room accompanied by his assistant, Ivan Passer. When the famous director looked at our table, he shouted excitedly: "Painmaker, the Painmaker! Painmaker! Ah, the Painmaker!" And he looked at Vladimír, sitting in the corner, and shouted again: "Remember? The Painmaker! Come on! That red-hot poker hovering over my knuckles?" And we all looked admiringly at Vladimír, wondering what magnificent event was waiting to be revealed. But Vladimír was nonplussed, and merely sat up, thrust out his hand, and Mr. Forman strode over to the table and seemed about to take Vladimír's hand but instead, he looked at Mr. Marysko sitting next to Vladimír, slouched under the weight of sexual and erotic problems. Mr. Forman sat down, put his arm around Marysko's shoulders, and began talking, addressing not only our table, but the neighboring tables as well: "Are you Mr. Marysko? You are! And did you teach music in Čáslav during the war? You did! Well, I was a student of yours, Miloš Forman, ten years old at the time. Gentlemen, we were practicing scales, and with each octave Mr. Marysko would gently rap me with a cane he called Painmaker. That's what he called it: the Painmaker. Once I said to him: 'Sir, I'm playing so badly because it's cold in here.' And Mr. Marysko said, 'Right, Forman. Go to the window and tell me what you see.' And I looked out the window at the town square and I said, 'Sir, I see a statue of the nation builder, Prince Ulicky.' And Mr. Marysko said: 'That is correct, Forman. And is there anything special about that statue?' And I said: 'He has no hands, because his enemies cut them off.' And Mr. Marysko said: 'Correct, Forman. And if you go on playing that way, that's how you'll end up. And now, it's time to practice. Another Painmaker is ready.' So I played my scales and Mr. Marysko pulled a red-hot poker out of the stove and held it above my fingers and roared: 'Since you're so cold, we have to warm those little knuckles up, just a tad ...'"

Mr. Forman addressed his story to the room, and everyone roared with laughter and congratulated Mr. Marysko, who now sat upright, basking in the glory. No one noticed that Vladimír was standing there, his hand still outstretched as it had been when Mr. Forman withdrew his. Vladimír stood there, gazing into the eye of some private disaster, paid his bill, and quietly slipped away, closing the door behind him, cutting off the sound of raucous laughter and shouts of "Painmaker! Painmaker! Painmaker!"

When Egon Bondy, who had just had eight teeth removed, heard about it, he was jubilant, rejoicing through his swollen cheeks. "Finally! Finally, poetic super-reality has turned off its miraculous taps and abandoned Vladimír. Finally, we've heard the last of his victorious laughter!"

Suddenly, he grew serious and in a voice full of portent, he said: "That's how I would have celebrated ten years ago, but not today, because what happened at the Tomcat is a kettle-drum overture to Vladimír's final symphony, but it's also a dr-umroll to what my tearful, restorative, and melancholy imagi-nation is telling me. Vladimír and I are two foci of the same ellipse, two axles on the same vehicle. We're a duly registered and incorporated firm, like Wichterle and Kovářík, like Laurin and Klement. Ay ay ay!" Egon Bondy was keening now, and he wrung his delicate white hands and thrust them into the dark air of the Bonaparte pub, and then, throwing his head back, he lamented quietly, and then, with abrupt and conductorly gestures, and following the Hasidic style of mourning prac-ticed in Galicia, he ripped all the buttons off his coat with a single yank to the lapels, then dumped an ashtray full of still-smoldering cigarette butts on his head, igniting his beautiful, sorrow-drenched hair and prompting one of the regulars to douse it with beer. "Goddamn it!" Egon said in a hoarse whis-per. "Vladimír, my sweet boy."

*

The morning after the night it happened, I saw the psychia-trist and head of the Suicide Help Line, Dr. Drvota, rushing up the steps in the courtyard. Even when he was still some distance away I could see the grief in his eyes. He rattled the door handle, then tapped on the window, shading his eyes with his hands as he peered through the glass to see if I was at home. I was standing in the doorway Vladimír and I had bricked up and then unbricked years ago. I was standing in the shadows, my heart pounding, watching his back as he went down the steps, then his torso, and finally, his head and his retreating hat. I lay down on the floor and listened to the past that came rushing back to me now, so rich and colorful, the past that became a tunnel, beginning with my first encounter with Vladimír on the Old Town Square at four o'clock in the morning. I was washing myself by the stone fish in the fountain, and so was Vladimír. There were gaps in the tunnel, stretches of time when we didn't see each other, only to meet again, reconnect, pick up where we left off. Lying on my back on the carpet, I saw that the tunnel was now ending, and that Vladimír, that night, had started his journey into the Universe along a runway he had long ago prepared for himself, for which he had rehearsed and gone into training.

Then someone else began pounding on the door, then on the window, and then back and forth from the door to the window, like two kettledrums at different pitches, and through the curtains I saw the anxious, ashen face of Vladimír's cousin, and she was radiating horror and dismay, the second confirmation that it was the end of Vladimír, and I knew that I couldn't get to my feet, that I could only lie there on my back and stare with unblinking eyes at the ceiling.

For a long time there was only silence. The sun was slipping down behind the high courtyard wall, dazzling and solemn, when into the sunlight ran Egon Bondy. He looked askance at the window and the locked door, then he knocked and called out, listened to the silence, then ran into the middle of the yard, turned around and spread his delicate arms wide, offering his hands and his pulsing veins to the sun, then he tilted his bearded, tousled head backward, haloed in light, redolent of Urquell, and cried out in a rapturous voice, like Doctor Ecstaticus: "Mein gutester Herr Vladimír! Now the knell has sounded for phenomenological anxieties. Now is the end of adaptation. Now neither existence nor imagination nor transcendence, nor even metaphysics, can concern you any longer. My dear Vladimír! Now you are flying straight to the place where the essence of nonhuman things, things necessary for humanity, lives and has its being. I take my leave of you, just for a while, because my sole consolation is in ontology, that invisible yet real kingdom you are now entering in a rocket ship more powerful by far than Apollo 12. You have no need to be sent into orbit first. You are flying direct, on the way to redemption, as the ancient but now dead God once interceded on our behalf. Monsieur Vladimír! I see you now, flying on your back, soaring straight into the center of an equilateral triangle, straight into the heart and headquarters of Being. Panie Wladimirze! Panie Wladimirze! Panie Wladimirze!"

"What's all that noise, what's all the shouting, waking up my kid!" Mrs. Slavíčková, a good mother, yelled down from her balcony. "Do you want my little Jeníček to go into seizures again?" She had truth on her side, the beautiful truth of a vigilant mother, just as Vladimír embodied the truth of the artists who came before us, just as I embodied truth lying motionless, paralyzed by grief, on the floor of my room, just as Egon Bondy embodied truth when, having transformed into Zbyněk Fišer, he shouted that truth from the launching pad in the courtyard of the Embankment of Eternity in Libeň.

Bohumil Hrabal
drypoint, 1953

Bohumil Hrabal reading "A Letter to Attendees at an Exhibition"
at the opening of the Boudník exhibition
at Galerie pod Radnicí, Ústí nad Orlicí, January 26, 1974

A Letter to Attendees at an Exhibition

To all of you who are reading this text and looking at Vladimír's graphics, don't think of them merely in terms of technique. Do not try to determine what Vladimír was trying to say about reality through his graphics. Think, as you look, about the miraculous effervescence of reality itself ticking away from second to second, and on into eternity.

Think about Vladimír, who felt at home wherever he was. Think of how his studio was always where he happened to be at the moment. Think of how he had the eyes of a child and those of a scientist as well, eyes that looked closely at what was around him, so that he imbued things of little apparent worth and meaning, things people scorn, with nobility and great beauty, though it may have been on a surface no larger than a handkerchief.

Those of you who aspire to become visual artists, don't wait until you have a studio and can live in Prague. Vladimír's studio was so small it could only accommodate three people; the fourth had to stand outside in the hallway. And yet, in that tiny room in Žižkov, Vladimír achieved, with his active graphics, work as important as what Jackson Pollock and Georges Mathieu accomplished with their gestural painting.

You who are simply observers should try, as Vladimír did, to peel back the skin of matter, to get inside the membranes that cover animate and inanimate forms. Don't be afraid to perform a vivisection, not just on yourself but on all things, because that is the only way you can find lifelong pleasure and rejoice in the knowledge that human eyes have evolved so that, through them, matter might see itself and recognize its own million-faceted beauty.

You who look at Vladimír's graphics should know that Vladimír was a trained lathe operator, that he loved all the expressive techniques afforded by this kind of work, and that he loved the materials from which useful objects and their constituent parts could be made. Vladimír thoroughly understood the workings of a lathe operator's workshop, and he was able to use those skills in his art in a way unique among graphic artists, to create artifacts so diverse, so beautiful, and so appealing.

His active graphics have the power to delight both the visual arts aesthete and the ironworker, the practitioner of the "black" trade. His lithographs can bear the closest scrutiny of the intellect as well as of the senses.

You who look upon Vladimír's graphic art, know that he could frighten me with his ability to spot materials and events that I had failed to notice. When he came across something exceptional, a surprised smile would appear on his face, I would look where he was looking until I saw what he saw. It could be anything: metal shavings, an overturned cart full of hardened asphalt, a wooden beam covered with dust, a blast furnace in the Poldi steel mills, a bird arcing through the air with a piece of straw in its beak.

Quite ordinary miracles and marvels were Vladimír's constant companions. When we had drunk our beer and were walking along a path above Vysočany, we'd sit down and while the trains thundered by below us, Vladimír would scrutinize the piles of coarse sand he'd gathered under his shoes as though he were looking down on earth from Skylab. He'd see hills and mountain ranges and talk about the glories of the Alps and the Pyrenees. He would rearrange the sand with his shoe and continue his ascent of the Andes and on into the Himalayas, without ever leaving the hillside in Vysočany.

When we'd go swimming by the towpath along the Vltava River in Libeň, Vladimír would often sit on the bottom step and wonder aloud why he should bother traveling the world when right here in Libeň, one could swim in the Black Sea or the Atlantic Ocean with no less delight than Rimbaud, who wrote "Le Bateau Ivre" sitting motionless in an ordinary riverboat.

You could never have found Vladimír in the famous Prague beer halls like the Golden Tiger or the Two Cats or U Pinkasů or U Schnellů. When I wanted to find him, I had to make the rounds of the taverns that were a complement of sorts to Vladimír's poetics. If he wasn't at the Bus Stop in Vysočany, I'd carry on to U Čižku, and if he wasn't there either, I'd look for him at the Chestnut Tree, and if I again came up empty, there was a faint chance he'd be drinking cheap beer in the stand-up bar at the Russian Court, and if he wasn't there I'd hop a streetcar and go looking for him in Žižkov, at the Rose Bush, where they'd tell me Vladimír hadn't been there for two days, but that I could certainly find him that evening, if not at

U Babiček, then at U Malvazu, where he ran the old windup gramophone. Sometimes he would hang out in Ludmila Street, at Hausman's, or one street over, at Přemysl's.

All of these taverns reeked of stale beer and the tablecloths bore vestiges of various debacles, spilled coffee and alcohol, and all of them had abominable pissoirs, though with such aesthetically rusted pipes and such beautiful waterfalls of hardened creosote splotched with canary-yellow urine that Vladimír would often stand there staring into a porcelain urinal filled with matches and cigarette butts mixed with balls of disinfectant and deodorant, and then cry out how wonderful it would be if he had the power and the art to push that entire creosote-covered wall through his lithographic press and turn it into a print.

On one occasion Vladimír and I came out of the Blue Star tavern and as we crossed to the other sidewalk Vladimír suddenly stopped. All I could see was his surprised and happy smile, and I felt a twinge of envy again. I knew that Vladimír had spotted something I had passed by every day and never noticed. Following his gaze, I saw several enormous metal letters mounted high up on the facade of a four-story building, letters that had caught his attention because they spelled KRÁSA – Beauty. I knew at once that it was a relic of the glory days of the Czech philosopher Ladislav Klíma, who had once lived at the Hotel Krása. Vladimír and I decided that early the next morning, we'd take those letters down and set them up in the Red Corner of the ČKD factory among the political posters, and if they wouldn't have them there, we would put them up in Mánes, the artists' club.

We returned the following day and were astonished to find

the letters gone. When we asked what had happened, we were told that workmen hired by the Housing Authority had taken the letters down and hauled them off to the scrapyard, lest they fall on the heads of passersby.

Again, all of you looking at Vladimír's graphic work, know that Vladimír was not disappointed, nor did he complain or curse those workers. Instead, for the rest of the day, he was in a state of apparent bliss over how they had managed to bring a beautiful story to such a gratifying conclusion. And so we went from tavern to tavern, on the lookout for more plots and follies that reality might spring on us.

Again, we were standing in the World Cafeteria, drinking their excellent beer, when I saw the familiar smile on Vladimír's face that told me he was looking at something extraordinary, so extraordinary, in fact, that he could no longer bear it and lowered his gaze. When he recovered, he stared again over my shoulder as if he couldn't believe his eyes, and this time the object of his admiration seemed to be something in the passage that led to the World Cinema. When I followed Vladimír's gaze, I saw a young Gypsy girl with a needle scratching something into the paint that covered a glass display window in the passageway.

Vladimír brought two glasses of beer and we carried them into the passageway, and what we saw there left us in awe. It was a gigantic mural that thousands of human hands had drawn and scraped into the paint that covered the window. Over several years, children and lovers and cinemagoers had scrawled images into the paint with coins or knives or needles or the edges of lipstick tubes, covering the entire glass wall with signs and symbols, initials and messages, most of them calligraphically beautiful, yet casually drawn, as one might doodle absentmindedly in the margins of a newspaper or school textbook. Vladimír spread his arms and declared that as soon as we'd saved enough money, we'd buy the entire beautiful pane of glass and take it home with us.

We scraped together a thousand crowns and the very next day, we went there and Vladimír, on entering the passageway, was already laughing his victorious laugh. When we reached the display window in the passageway, we saw a painter kneeling on the floor, carefully painting over the last of the graffiti. The entire glass wall had been gessoed and primed with enamel, like a canvas, like a tabula rasa, so that everything could begin all over again.

All of you who admire Vladimír's graphic works, know that such small incidents can happen to you, and if you think of them as a part of your destiny, as a remarkable and fateful encounter, you too will begin to regard your life as exceptional and therefore beautiful.

Once, Vladimír and I went to Pikovice to visit his aunt. When we got off the train and saw the muddy, swollen Sázava river, we quickly stripped down and slipped into the fast-flowing current. The late-spring floodwaters carried us downstream with the speed of a racing bike, the hilltops and roads sweeping backward past us. Vladimír was radiant, and when the spring floodwaters carried us surging forward over the place where there would normally be a weir, he laughed his victorious laugh. Then, when the river had carried us more than a kilometer away from our clothes, it swept us into a quiet backwater and we climbed out and walked back upstream and made one more magnificent voyage down the river.

Vladimír had only one regret. As we were being carried over the weir, he said he'd have found it more exciting if a nail had ripped a small gash in his leg so he could have physically experienced what the painter Alberto Burri experienced when he first deliberately slashed a canvas. Then he added that he couldn't have everything he wanted, and that he was satisfied with experiencing what the matrix must experience when he ran it through the rotogravure press and it came out the other side.

That was a beautiful time in his life, when he was able to compress into his graphic art expressions that were commensurate with his vision.

Back then, Vladimír and I went to Nymburk by motorcycle. I could only make my Perak, a Jawa 250, go so fast, but Vladimír enjoyed telling the story of riding the Perak with me down a trail through the woods along the Labe River. Driving over some dunes, I went into a skid and I remember Vladimír flying over me and sliding headfirst into a clump of bushes that swallowed him up so that only the soles of his shoes were visible. Horrified, I ran around the thicket yelling, "Vladimír! For God's sake, are you all right?"

I found him lying in the sand with a lump on his forehead, convulsed with laughter and excitement, yelling that I'd made his day. His tumble into the bushes inspired him to do a whole collection of lithographs, just for me.

The most beautiful series of monotypes, however, about thirty-five large pieces that form the final phase of Vladimír's work, was inspired by a ride on a Jawa 500, driven by a lathe operator called Kotrč, with whom Vladimír came to see me in Nymburk, crammed into the tiny sidecar as in a sitz bath. Inspired by that single ride and aided by a modest loan, Vladimír worked exclusively for Mr. Kotrč for two days, on condition that Mr. Kotrč buy him inks and keep him supplied with jugs of beer for those forty-eight hours. Mr. Kotrč was a small, timorous man of few words, and he had a terrible battle with his wife for permission to hang a single lithograph from that series of thirty-five on the wall.

All of you who look with wonder at Vladimír's art, know that Vladimír, though a proletarian, was an aristocrat whose life invites all those who think life is worth living to the full to follow him. If you dive headfirst, with audacity, into the unrepeatable present, you will find yourselves in the very heart of eternity.

Recollections, Bildsalat
drypoint with active graphics, 1955

Wedding announcement for Dr. Hrabal
aquatint, 1956

Fish
drypoint with the active technique, 1955

Fiery Women
drypoint, 1955

Coral Reef
active graphics, 1960

18/200   Reichlich 1957 X.

Explosionalism
active graphics, 1967

Untitled
structural graphics, 1959

Translator's afterword

B ohumil Hrabal wrote *The Gentle Barbarian* at a strange time
in his country's tumultuous history. It was five years after
the Soviet invasion and occupation of Czechoslovakia in 1968,
five years into a process the Communist Party called "normal-
ization," five years that saw the slow, steady suffocation of free
expression, when the public voices of hundreds of writers, including Hrabal's, were silenced.

It was a period when an eerie calm seemed to have settled
over the visible surface of life. And yet the calm was deceptive,
for if five years had been enough time for a repressive regime to
reassert its control, it was also enough time for creative people
to find ways to push back, and by 1973 there were clear signs
that this was beginning to happen. I was living in Prague then,
teaching English and drawn into a budding underground art
and music scene that was just one of many examples of creative
resistance. Another was the widespread growth of "samizdat,"
the spontaneous, unofficial "publishing" of handmade books
and journals meant to circumvent censorship. It was in the early
stages of this life-giving renaissance that *The Gentle Barbarian*
first appeared.

After Vladimír Boudník's death in December 1968 at the age of forty-four, a group of those who knew him and loved him created an informal association, the Society of Friends of Vladimír Boudník, dedicated to promoting the work and the legacy of a man they regarded not just as a friend, but as an important protagonist of Czech postwar art. To honor his memory and celebrate what would have been his fiftieth birthday in 1974, they arranged for two exhibitions of his work and undertook to publish a samizdat volume of excerpts from Boudník's journals from the early 1950s, together with contributions from people who had known him. In the fall of 1973, Hrabal was asked to write something for the volume. He came up with a short memoir called "A Journal Written at Night."

"As I was writing," Hrabal recalled later, "I was inundated by so many memories of the years I spent with those gentle barbarians, Vladimír and Egon Bondy, that I had to write another piece." That other piece became the main section of this book.

In early 1974, Hrabal wrote "A Letter to Attendees at an Exhibition," which he read at the opening of the second Boudník exhibition in Ústí nad Orlicí in January 1974. Hrabal added that letter to the first two pieces and in early February, he put into circulation five bound typescripts he titled *The Gentle Barbarian: Educational Texts*. He also included a manifesto called "Abdication," issued in the early 1950s by a group of avant-garde artists and writers who wished to distance themselves from Stalinist cultural policies. (Since Hrabal did not write it, we have not included it in this translation.)

In the fall of 1974, one of the more "established" samizdat publishers, Edice Petlice, run by the Czech dissident writer Ludvík Vaculík, brought out twenty copies of the book, to which Hrabal had added two more sections, including the scene at the Tomcat pub with the film director Miloš Forman. A year later, Václav Havel's samizdat venture, Edice Expedice, published the book as well.

All of these volumes, typed and bound in hard covers, spawned an indeterminable number of further copies, most of which would have passed from hand to hand, giving the book a readership far greater than the number of copies in circulation would suggest. In the illicit, underground world of samizdat, *The Gentle Barbarian*, without benefit of publicity or marketing, became a kind of "bestseller."

Not everyone who knew Boudník well was entirely happy with what Hrabal had written. In his 2009 biography of Boudník, his close friend Vladislav Merhaut cautions that *The Gentle Barbarian* "is not the literature of fact." While Merhaut loved the book, he also felt that Hrabal had let his representation of Boudník as a "brilliant lunatic with grand ambitions" overshadow the substance, importance, and above all, the evolution of Boudník's work.

Tomáš Mazal, who published an extensive biography of Bohumil Hrabal in 2004, agrees that Hrabal may have fictionalized some incidents, but after conversations with Hrabal and Egon Bondy (who claimed that Hrabal's representation of him was total fiction), Mazal concluded that the incidents and conversations in the book "more or less happened," though they are often rendered with a degree of "poetic license."

As if to anticipate such caveats, Hrabal's brief prologue to this book suggests that his account is both *"Dichtung und Wahrheit*, poetry and truth," a phrase he borrowed from one of his favorite authors, Goethe. It's a description that could be applied to most of Hrabal's work. "I always write about the strange things that have happened to me and the enviable things that have happened to others, so my point of departure is always what's authentic," Hrabal told an interviewer in 1983. "But the playfulness in me compels me, with a certain degree of imagination, to rearrange the order of events, to sprinkle into that authenticity the yeast of a fantasy that makes things more precisely what they are, just as the juice of the grape is transformed into wine, or the wort into beer. I call this chemical reaction *pábení*. Only when *pábení* is present does a piece of writing begin to effervesce, to ferment."

Pábení has sometimes been translated as "palavering," suggesting that the main hallmarks of Hrabal's style are rambling monologues and the "found" conversations of ordinary people that he weaves into his work. Yet for Hrabal, *pábení* is more than style, it's a quality intrinsic to the writing itself, like poetry. The "truth" of *The Gentle Barbarian* is inseparable from Hrabal's telling of it.

*

Bohumil Hrabal could be a notoriously fast writer, and literary translation can be a notoriously slow process. What took Hrabal weeks to write took me months to translate, though the work was spread out over two years, and included two trips to the Czech Republic, several walks through Libeň (where, I can report, "the World" complex is still standing, dusty, derelict, and boarded up, awaiting another Mr. Svět to restore it to its former glory), and many conversations and consultations with friends and colleagues.

Thanks to my fellow translators Mike Baugh, Derek Paton, Justin Quinn, Gerald Turner, and Alex Zucker, who were always ready with suggestions on how to render typically difficult Czechisms into English. Special thanks to Jakub Chrobák, Tomáš Mazal, Zbyšek Sion, and Lucie Tucková, for their willingness to spend hours with me explaining some of the more difficult passages in the book, to Vladislav Merhaut for clarifying Boudník's graphic techniques, the chronology of his life, and the origins of this book, and to Jiří Gruntorad, founder of the Libri Prohibiti collection of Czech samizdat, for valuable bibliographical information. Jan Placák generously provided the scans of some of Boudník's work from his private collection.

My thanks as well to Declan Spring and his colleagues at New Directions for their belief in this book, their championing of Hrabal's work, and making a place for him in their pantheon of great writers.

I owe a special debt of gratitude to Drenka Willen, for bringing her years of editorial expertise, her deep understanding of Central European sensibility, and her ear for a good sentence, to the final stages of this translation.

Finally, my deepest thanks to my wife, Patricia Grant, for her editorial assistance and constant support in so many other ways, and to our dear friend Marketa Goetz-Stankiewicz, for her encouragement and love.

*

I'd like to dedicate this translation to the memory of an old friend, Jan Steklík, who died in 2017 at the age of seventy-nine in his hometown of Ústí nad Orlicí, where Boudník's work was shown in 1973 and 1974. Honza was a fiercely independent artist and cartoonist with an endlessly playful imagination. Like many in his generation, Honza knew and was a great admirer of Boudník, and like Boudník, he was a living example of how to embrace life and art as a seamless continuum.

Vladimír Boudník

Born in Prague on March 17, 1924, Vladimír Boudník trained as a tool and die maker before being deployed to Germany in 1943, when his country was occupied by the Nazis. Forced to work in a steel mill in Dortmund, he survived heavy allied bombing of the city, and later wrote: "I saw dozens of churches reduced to rubble, hundreds of paintings and statues destroyed, libraries burnt to the ground. I dreamed of making the kind of art that would outlast any catastrophe." After his return to Prague in 1944, he enrolled in the State Graphic School, and in 1949, he issued two manifestoes arguing for an approach to art he called "Explosionalism." He began testing his ideas in the streets of Prague by inviting onlookers to create images based on cracks and blotches on the walls. He continued these "actions," often considered forerunners of "happenings," until 1957.

Boudník lived as a subtenant of Bohumil Hrabal in the Prague working-class district of Libeň from 1950 to 1952. Over the course of his career, he experimented with different graphic techniques, and developed several new and original approaches to creating lithographs. Long a cult hero among his peers, he was just beginning to gain wider recognition, both at home and abroad, when his life ended tragically in December 1968.